In the Doorway of the Church

Living on the Street

Eli J. Elliott

Thanks to my mother and father for guiding and trusting me through this adventure called life

Contents

Introduction

> Consider it all joy, my brethren, when you encounter various trials, knowing that the testing of your faith produces endurance. And let endurance have its perfect result, so that you may be perfect and complete, lacking in nothing.
>
> James 1:2–4

We see all through the book of James that we, as Christians, will be tested. Have you ever wondered what happens to those of us who don't pass the tests and trials that are put in our paths? I fear that I know all too well what happens from my personal life. If you are anything like me, you also know that if we fail the test that God gives us, we will see that same test pop up in the near future. God is a very patient teacher, but I am afraid that He's also just. We will never be mature Christians if we can't pass trials that are placed on our path. If we are repeating the same test over and over again, shouldn't that tell us we should do something different? The testing of our faith is not always fun, and it can be tricky.

When we think of these tests and trials, we think of the hard ones that make us stronger, like overcoming an addiction or running into money problems, but rarely do we think of God testing us when something good happens. In James 1:9, the author states, "But the brother of humble circumstances is to glory in his high position." Pride makes us boastful of what the Lord has given us. Whenever we receive a blessing from God, whether material or not, we often think of it as just that: a blessing that God wants us to enjoy. While this is true, we should also consider whether this blessing is also a test. It might be an oxymoron to say something is a good trial, but I think it gets the point across. God is definitely interested in what we do with what He gives to us, great or small.

God desires us to be wise with the blessings He has given to us. He also desires for men and women to be saved. In this whole world, only the souls of mankind will make it to heaven. That is an investment that will never lose value. Ever.

Invest in man!

The question we must ask based on this information is, what are we doing with the blessings (or tests) that God has given us? Are we using them to invest in the souls of mankind, or are we maxing out our income to reflect a lifestyle that fits our desires? When I was house shopping a few years ago, the real estate agent suggested that we buy the most expensive house we could afford. Of course he was a salesman, but his logic was that we would always get raises, so even if we were maxed out when we bought the house, it would not be for long. Unfortunately, many people think like this and start digging themselves into a financial hole that forces them to only give to their debt.

Again, if you are anything like I am, you spend the majority of your time making money to meet your budget, and that's fine—we are commanded to work to support ourselves. But when the possessions that we have and the desire to have them enslave us to pay for them, a problem can arise. The problem is that we easily get so busy working for our possessions that when we have time to spend investing in man, we want to rest from our hard work and enjoy the luxuries it has provided. James 4:14 tells us that life is like a vapor. As morbid as it sounds, our lives are going to be over soon, and this home that we have on earth is not worth investing everything we have.

If we do pass the tests that God has for us, and if we want to follow Him and take up our cross, then one more question remains: How? How are we to invest in mankind? I do not have all the answers, but I learned some very valuable hints when it comes to serving others in need, whether physically, mentally, or spiritually. The lessons that I learned during my time on the streets can translate into how to love and serve people from all walks of life.

You will find examples of people who were effective in ministry, and you will see examples of people who were not so effective in ministry. You will see a perspective on how well the church and individuals are serving the homeless that you perhaps have never seen before.

Chapter 1

The Time Before

Have you ever wondered where your next meal is going to come from? Have you ever wondered where you were going to sleep and if you would be safe that night? Have you ever wondered when your next shower would be? Have you ever felt what it is like to be away from everyone who cares about you and not know when or if you would see them again? Some of you may have felt these things, or some of you may be just like I was. Never, in my life, had I dealt with any of those issues. I grew up in the Bible Belt of the wealthiest country in the world with a loving Christian family that took care of me physically, emotionally, and spiritually. Don't get me wrong: I thank God for the way I was raised and where He had me; but, at one point in my life, I wished that my upbringing had been different. It would have been easier, in some ways, not to have the luxuries that a middle-class US citizen could enjoy. That way, I would know that being a Christian was real and not simply a way of life. But who am I to question where God placed me in the world?

Even though I had everything that I needed growing up, I wanted to get a glimpse of what it would be like if I had nothing. I wanted to give up the luxuries that I had in order to fully trust God to take care of me. I wanted to be forced to trust God like never before. I've been on mission trips in the United States and internationally and, every now and then, I saw missionaries limit their ministry by living financially above the people they were ministering to. I spoke with some of the natives, and they told me that they did not understand how someone could be a Christian and not be making disciples. One of the main factors was that the missionaries could not relate to the native people because they were nothing like them. They didn't know what it was like to live without their luxuries. This is part of what Paul means when he says that he became all things to all people. When ministering to people who are different from us, we should give up anything that hinders us from serving them. I never want material luxuries to get in the way of making disciples.

During the last part of my freshmen year of college, I kept reading over the passage of scripture about the rich young ruler in Mark 10:17–23:

> As He was setting out on a journey, a man ran up to Him and knelt before Him, and asked Him, "Good Teacher, what shall I do to inherit eternal life?" And Jesus said to him, "Why do you call Me good? No one is good except God alone. You know the commandments, 'Do not murder, Do not commit adultery, Do not steal, Do not bear false witness, Do not defraud, Honor your father and mother.'" And he said to Him, "Teacher, I have kept all these things from my youth up." Looking at him, Jesus felt a love for him and said to him, "One thing you lack: go and sell all you possess and give to the poor, and you will have treasure in heaven; and come, follow Me." But at these words he was saddened, and he went away grieving, for he was one who owned much property. And Jesus, looking around, said to His disciples, "How hard it will be for those who are wealthy to enter the kingdom of God!"

Who is to say that God does not do that anymore? We know that Jesus was after the rich young ruler's heart, but this is a genuine technique for reaching a man's heart and soul. Nearly every time I hear this passage preached, no one seems to think that God asks people to give up their possessions and follow Him. Preachers often say to search for whatever is holding you back from a pure relationship with Christ and get rid of it. But what if someone is just like the rich young ruler and loves riches too much? Would that be foolish? Foolish or not, God used this passage to give direction to my life.

Although I may not be considered rich in comparison to some, I did like my stuff. For me to give up my possessions and to do without would teach me to let go of what I thought I needed and let God show me how to trust Him fully. God used all these things to show me what I needed to do.

I love listening to music in the car. I was on the two-hour drive from my hometown to school, and I was singing out loud (unless, of course, I came into a little town, at which point I acted cool, just in case someone was looking). Suddenly, I felt great conviction in my heart about talking to God; I felt like God was saying, "Let's talk." But that would mean turning off my music! And a car ride without music seems so much longer. As simple as it should have been, it was still hard for me to cut the music and talk to God. I ended up turning it off, and I started to pray. I already had all these things running around in my head and I wanted to learn how to best serve God by ministering to others. My prayer was (and still is) that God would use my life to make the biggest impact possible on this world for Christ's name's sake. I can't explain where it came from other than God just putting this idea in my head. He led me to live a homeless life for a while. I did not know when or for how long, but I knew that I had to do it. So I said, "Yes, Lord, I am willing."

Despite what I probably should have thought about it (like, "God you know I could die"), I was really excited. I thought that it would be a neat thing to do. It would be hard, but I thought that people would think it was radical and a little out of the ordinary and it would give them something to talk about. You get the idea. God called me to humble myself by getting rid of my possessions and relying on Him, and it took no time for it to go to my head. Pride comes in wealth and also in poverty. All the hype about doing something cool left me the first moment I set foot on the streets, and God took my pride away in an instant, but that's a story for later.

In order to do something like this, I didn't need very much: I just needed to have no other responsibilities. While I was at a Passion conference in Atlanta, God began to speak to me, again, in silence. This was in April of 2008. He made me realize that the summer would be perfect for me to live homeless. I was surprised because I honestly did not expect to have to do it that soon. Now was the time to start getting ready. There were not many physical things I needed to prepare, but mentally, I needed to be ready. So I started telling everyone what I was going to do. The first person I called was my mom. I did not know any other way to tell her the news than to just say it. I told her that God was calling on me to live homeless on the streets for the summer and that I would not have a phone, money, or anything that a homeless person would not have (although some of them had a few items). I waited on the phone to hear her reply. Silence was all that I heard. Eventually, I heard her trying to hold back her tears, and I gave her a while before I started talking again. She informed me that she and my dad were praying for me the night before and asking God to reveal to me what He would have me do that summer, but I don't think this was the answer that she was looking for. As hard as it was for her to hear that from me, she and my dad supported me through it because they knew that it was what God wanted me to do.

After the news got out about what I would be doing, people started asking me questions or offering advice. Some people thought I was crazy, while others did not see how this could be God's will for my life. Most of my friends told me about what their parents said. That's where I heard some crazy comments. People didn't usually call me stupid to my face, but I would hear through the grapevine that someone thought what I was doing was foolish. Was it a wise choice to put myself in danger when God had obviously provided a good home for me to stay in? Was it smart to eat out of a trash can or sleep outside with who-knows-who walking beside me? Yes! It was so logical to me. I fear God. I have a fear of having a normal, lukewarm, American-dream life that deep down asks, "Is there something more out there?" A mediocre Christian life that feels sort-of-kind-of satisfied about the day that the Lord has made—that, dear friends, is what I fear. The Christian life is not always a safe life in the world's standards. To say we believe that the Christian life is always safe makes me question if we understand scripture enough for it to change our lives.

The next question that I had for God was this: "Where do you want me to do this, Lord?" I could have gotten frustrated with God because He didn't really let me know right away, or I could have gotten so bogged down with trying to find the right place that I would delay the trip or even cancel it altogether. God gave me an answer, though. Maybe He did so out of frustration, but nonetheless, He did. The answer was simple: "It doesn't matter where you do it!" I learned that doing nothing and waiting on a crystal clear answer from God is not always right. You have heard the saying, "If I say 'jump,' you say, 'how high?'" It's good to ask "How high?" and to seek direction from God, but I wonder if we sometimes ask God too many questions. How high? Do you want me to hold my breath or close my eyes? Want me to jump with two feet or one? As silly as that sounds, I wonder how ridiculous our excuses sound to God. All I needed to do was jump. Sometimes our lives are like that. When we could be busy doing God's work, we instead waste time thinking of all these questions. Sometimes I imagine God with His head buried in His hands, shaking His head and wanting to scream, "If I say 'jump,' JUST DO IT!" So, that being said, I decided that I would start in Atlanta because that was a big enough city to support a homeless person.

Although I did not want to sit around and waste time, I did want to go about this in the wisest way possible. I know it seems contradictory. Can anyone possibly make a wise choice about something that sounds so foolish? My friends at school informed me that I was not the first to do this and gave me a book about a guy who did the same thing. What more could I ask for? Here was a guideline for me to go by. I devoured the book in a few days, and I felt some of the same things that he felt before starting. Two things stuck out to me while reading this book: (1) he went to people to give him advice, and (2) he had a partner go with him. I did not really know who to talk to about advising me on this. It was actually a little easier to ask someone to do it with me than to ask for advice. If you knew some of my friends, you would understand.

I asked a few different guys if they would like to join me. The ones that really wanted to go did not end up doing it, mainly because their parents didn't let them. I searched online to try to meet someone or get a large Christian organization to advertise or something—anything really. That did not happen either. I just knew for sure that God had someone for me. A friend of the family stopped by a week or so before I left, and she told me that she prayed that I would have someone to be my companion through this time. I thought for sure that this was a sign straight from God. You know those little signs I'm talking about. After that, I honestly felt that God would provide me with someone at the last minute. Little did I know that God had very different plans for me.

The next thing I wanted to do was to find out as much as I could about homeless life in Atlanta. I wanted to know where to go and where not to go. I got in touch with a friend of a friend who worked in homeless ministry in downtown Atlanta for eleven years. He was the director of a resource center called City of Refuge. I got on their website and tried to learn all I could about what they did. I called him up and asked if he had any advice for me. His advice was priceless. He asked me to reconsider doing anything like that. He even offered me an internship at City of Refuge and said that they would take care of me. We ended up coming to somewhat of a compromise. I would stay there for a few days and learn a little bit about homeless life, without being thrown straight into it.

Another friend called me when she found out what I was doing and told me that I had to meet her niece. She explained to me that Bethany, her niece, lived close to downtown Atlanta and ministered to the poor in her community. She said that, if nothing else, it would be a good idea to talk with her on the phone. After a game of phone tag, Bethany and I ended up chatting about how God led me to do this. I wanted for us to meet sometime while I was there so that I could vent or just relax in good company. I did not want to be cut off from the body of Christ for that long—especially during such a trying time. I found out about a weekly college meeting at a nearby church, and I planned to attend it to stay sane.

I visited many friends and family before I left, as if I was saying good-bye for good. It could have been for good, as far as I knew. I was visiting one of my great-uncles when God spoke to me. We were reading scripture and praying together. I do not remember what was read before or after these verses, but Acts 21:11–13 gave me the encouragement and confidence to keep going. Paul was returning to Jerusalem when a prophet named Agabus came to him and forcefully warned him not to go back to Jerusalem because he would be bound and handed over to the Gentiles. Everyone around Paul started begging him to stay, but Paul said that he was ready to be bound and even die for the Lord's sake.

Not everyone was discouraging me from going, but a quite a few people were. Actually, the person that had the most experience told me not to do it, but these few verses pushed me to keep on, not because I thought that I was big and bad and could take it, but because I knew that it would be for Christ's name's sake. I was actually beginning to see just how small I really was. I was mentally on the way to being prepared for this journey, but it's not something that you can really get prepared for.

God had provided two contacts for me to learn about what life on the streets was like and to encourage me. I had a plan to stay at City of Refuge for a few days before I hit the streets. I was planning on leaving June 1 and coming back August 1, simply to give others some sort of structure. These dates were just guidelines. God was giving me the encouragement and power to face what was ahead of me. I still did not have a partner and it was only a day away, but I didn't lose hope that I would get one.

There was only one thing left to do: pack. I needed to pack for two months' worth of living. I was wearing jeans and a T-shirt. I packed one pair of shorts and a jacket, my Bible, journal, and a book. I also had a sleeping bag and about thirty dollars (which lasted longer than I thought). I took a few odds and ends like duct tape, a harmonica, a pocket knife, and my ID. My hiking pack got heavy quickly. I had very little for a two-month trip, and I got rid of more than half of what I had the first few days out on the streets.

A dear friend of mine wanted to do something special for me before I left. The night before I left, she wanted to have a dinner and prayer service at my church for me. Again, God was using others to encourage me and soak me in prayer before I went out. I was around many people whom I loved, but the feeling that I had was strange to me. I'm not sure if I seemed distant to the others, but I felt a bit disconnected or detached from the world. My mind was probably overanalyzing everything. I was not unhappy by any means, but for the first time, I was beginning to feel nervous. I believe that it is completely normal to feel kind of bogged down just before something big is going to take place. For me, it always seems that the valley comes right before the mountain. This is nothing new, but to hear it and to experience it are two very separate things.

On May 31, my family and I left for Atlanta. On the way there, we stopped in Athens, Georgia, to meet two guys who used to live on the streets. They now serve the Lord by feeding the homeless people they used to live with. One of my friends wanted me to meet them and get any advice that I could get from them. The first thing that these two men told me was not to do it. I hear it yet again from people who know what they are talking about. After they found out that this is what God wanted me to do and that I was going to do it no matter what, they suggested for me to follow through but to stay there in Athens for safety reasons. I'm a skinny white dude who was about to go to a city where I would be picked on and very possibly harmed by simply being there and because of the color of my skin. I'm sure that my parents loved hearing all this.

After talking with them for a while, we left to go give some of the homeless people food and pillows. The first place that we came to was a tent city. Basically, a tent city is a place where homeless people live in tents on a few acres of woods. In this place, someone built a few small shelters for the people to stay in. They were just big enough to fit two twin mattresses. There was a small campfire there, and the mosquitoes were as bad as the smell.

We began to introduce ourselves to the people who lived there. All sorts of thoughts were going through my head. I felt sort of out of it. My heart was burdened for them. I was a bit quiet because I didn't know what to say. I wanted so badly to do more than what I was doing, but I did not know what else to do. The amount of drama was unreal. The police were there when we got there. I got a glimpse of what I would be living in. We also went under a bridge where some others were. I don't think that I have ever been anywhere that dirty before. The smell was almost unbearable—urine mixed with people that don't bathe and garbage. All sorts of questions of doubt came back to me, but I couldn't give up. Besides, I had already invested fifteen whole minutes packing for this trip.

God was still preparing me for what was coming—and not only me but my parents as well. I spent one more night with my family before June 1. We all stayed with a couple that my parents know in Atlanta. More friends came and stayed the night as well. They fed me well, and the food was already beginning to taste better than ever. The plan was to go to the City of Refuge on Sunday morning for their worship service and meet some of the people there. That is when I would say good-bye.

Overall, I did this for one reason: God told me to. If my intentions were to do it in order to do something radical, I would have failed miserably. My intentions did sway a little due to the way I was being talked about, but when the rubber met the road (or sneakers hit the sidewalk), any false intentions went out the window. I did not care about being radical, being different, or doing something cool. There was only one reason I was going to stay there: I was there because God was with me. Anything shy of that would have made it wrong. Despite how clearly God spoke to me, I honestly started asking myself some of the same questions people had asked me: Did I hear you correctly, Lord? Am I crazy or stupid? Will I die? All these things were going through my head.

Chapter 2

Where Do I Eat?

> If God is willing to ask us to do His will, knowing that we can and will fail if we try on our own power, then how much more should we put our faith and trust in Him and just *do* as He says and *go* where He leads, trusting in His strength and power?
>
> Matthew 16:24

Day 1

I didn't sleep well on my last night in a bed even though I was surrounded by people whom I know and love. This day came fast. Most of my friends were going on different mission trips all over the world for the summer, and I was going to be two and half hours away from home. I was so close to home, yet I was already feeling very far away. After a huge breakfast, I said good-bye to my friends. My parents and I left for City of Refuge. It sounds kind of ironic, come to think of it: I was going to a place called City of Refuge to start my journey of life on the streets of Atlanta.

When we arrived, my parents and I sat through the church service that Sunday, patiently waiting to meet the staff. The director was preaching on this particular Sunday, and I remember him telling the congregation that he moved into a place that was dangerous to live even though he had a family to take care of. I can remember him saying that his house got broken into numerous times. He, like me and probably anyone in this type of ministry, had people tell him that they did not think he was making a wise choice. Even when the director did not see a lot of results, he knew that he was there because he was called to serve. He took his family into greater danger because God called him there and stood his ground when people had the nerve to tell him that it was not the right thing to do. I think some of the naysayers mean to say that they really care about you and don't want you to get hurt, or they wish that they had the courage to respond to God's call even if it put them in danger. Life is just pressing in on them, and they vent their frustration on things or people they do not understand. There are more reasons I'm sure, but you get the point. My mind was bursting with thoughts, but my emotions were dry.

After the church service ended, my family and I met some of the staff at City of Refuge. Only the director was expecting me, and he was on his way out of town. He introduced me to Seth, the guy I would be staying with for the next few days. Seth was in charge of a house where other guys in a program at City of Refuge are living. Seth said that I would have a spot on the couch. I guess this was God's way of lowering me into the cold water. I was minutes away from leaving my parents and younger siblings, but still, for some reason, my emotions felt so bland. Seth had to leave to take some of the kids home, and he would not be back to take me to the house for another half hour, so I decided to ride with him to get my journey started. All the weeks of preparation and time with each other was wrapped up in a moment. I gave my parents a good-bye, an "I love you," and a big hug, and I tossed my bag into the fifteen-passenger van full of loud kids. We drove off, and I waved to my parents.

I was looking out of the window of the van, staring at this unfamiliar place. The thoughts returned. "I'm crazy. What am I doing? This place does not look safe at all." That was because it wasn't. I was later informed not to walk on the streets after dark. We were a few miles outside of downtown Atlanta on the west side of town. This was the area I needed to avoid because of the color of my skin. These were the things that I needed to learn while I was at City of Refuge.

> "Behold, I send you out as sheep in the midst of wolves; so be shrewd as serpents and innocent as doves" (Matthew 10:16).

It was somewhat boring at the house where Seth lived with three others. One of the housemates was Ryan. Ryan had spent some time on the streets. When he came in, I was (halfway) sleeping on the couch in the small living room next to the kitchen. I overheard Ryan and Seth talking about what I was doing there. When Seth explained what I was doing and why, Ryan did not think that it was the best idea, to say the least. Having lived on the streets, he knew more than Seth about life "out there." Seth tried to convince Ryan that he thought I would be fine, but Ryan wasn't so sure.

Later that night, I had a chance to talk to Ryan. He informed me that he was not going to be staying there much longer. In fact, he planned to be out in a few days. Ryan had two kids to take care of and not much money, but he offered to take me somewhere nice to eat when I was done for the summer. Although he is a Christian now, Ryan shared some of his history with me—and it was different from anything I ever experienced. He grew up in Ohio, where he was involved in gangs. He told me a few of the things that he used to do, but now he knows that he is forgiven. Ryan's life was anything but easy, and yet he freely gave what he could to help me in any way. He gave me his number and told me to call him if I was in any kind of trouble. He even offered to spend a couple of nights out there with me. Keep in mind that I was still looking for someone to go with me. I had my eyes open, but Ryan was not the one. After Ryan talked to me, he was convinced that this was God's will for me and gave me his support, but living on the streets was not for him. I was now a little frightened because he told me just how dangerous it would be.

Ryan does not hold a high position in a church. He is not a pastor or a teacher of any kind, but I had learned more from him than anyone else to that point. God was teaching me just how important it is to listen to others, no matter what their status. We can learn just as much from the quiet person that sits in the back of the church, or even sleeps in the park, as we can from the leaders of our church.

Later I met the rest of the people working at City of Refuge to learn how they provide support to people below the poverty level. They have a food pantry for low-income households, where I helped out a little bit. I also hung out in the lobby to try to meet some of people that I might be living with on the streets. While there, I was introduced to a man named Dread who hung around City of Refuge and would help out occasionally.

Dread is an easygoing middle-aged man. I noticed that he was limping a little bit, and one of the workers asked him to share his story with me. He sat down with me and began to explain that he has seen the goodness of God. He rarely looked at me while speaking. Dread was shot to the ground three weeks before I met him. I can't remember why, but according to him, it was not his fault. He almost bled to death on the sidewalk. He explained to me how the anger that built up inside of him was outrageous. Even while he was in the hospital, all he could think about was revenge. He made plans to buy a gun, find the man that shot him, and do the same in return.

When Dread got out of the hospital, he set out to do exactly what he had planned. He bought a gun and began his search for the man who caused him so much pain. He wanted that man dead. He eventually found the man and pointed the gun at him. This is where he said that he saw the goodness of God. He intended to shoot the man, but he said that something came over him and all he said was, "I love you and I forgive you," and then he walked away.

I'm not sure if Dread is homeless or if he was even telling the truth, but he showed me the scars and staples on his side from surgery, which looked legitimate. He mentioned to me that he still loves and forgives the man who shot him. He kept explaining to me that he has seen the goodness of God. "Bless those who persecute you, bless and do not curse" (Romans 12:14). To hear stories like that is truly amazing to me. I had to ask myself if I could do the same thing. Dread gave me an idea of what I was getting into.

My prayer had been that God would make me great for His cause. Let's pause here for a minute—I knew what I was praying for. You may have heard the "don't ask for patience" joke. While understanding the joke, it saddens me when Christians take it seriously. I knew, in the back of my mind, that God was going to break me in order for His greatness to shine through. I prayed that He would break me, and my prayers were answered. I am not afraid to pray for God to mold me, whatever that means, and I hope that you're not either. This world needs Christians who are not scared of praying for things that can and will cause trials. I fear what will happen to me if I don't pray for difficult things. I refuse to live a life that *could* have been great. "Consider it all joy, my brethren, when you encounter various trials, knowing that the testing of your faith produces endurance. And let endurance have its perfect result, so that you may be perfect and complete, lacking in nothing" (James 1:2–4). I was learning how to be great in God's eyes. We have to humble ourselves and be obedient to be great, just like Jesus's example for us (Philippians 2:5–8). I had to serve others and be last. In God's eyes, we work our way down in order to obtain greatness.

While I was at City of Refuge, I did not have any real responsibility, which was another good picture of what I was getting into, but it also allowed me time to study scripture. In between studying, I helped out as much as possible while learning everything I could about the homeless in Atlanta.

Day 3

By Tuesday, I had helped unload sixty-five thousand pairs of shoes off of the truck. I was just helping do whatever they needed me to do. As I spent more time in the lobby where people received their food, I was able to get a glimpse of how unappreciative people were.

Here was this resource center giving food away, and most of the people were still complaining about anything and everything. I was astonished at their responses. How could someone complain while they are getting something for free? It was beyond me. Who could be so unappreciative of a free gift? Do I appreciate the gifts God gives to me? As Philippians 2:14 tell us, do *everything* without complaining or arguing.

One of the main reasons I picked Atlanta was because of the sizeable homeless population that exists in the city. I figured that someone was feeding them, and now I needed to find out where to eat from day to day. City of Refuge handed out food on the streets in a few different locations, so I rode with Seth and made the deliveries to find out where to eat. I was trying to remember how to get to each location, but there were so many streets that I couldn't tell them apart. By the look of these streets, I could tell this was not a place I wanted to be at night. At that point, I still had no clue where I would be living, but I was almost positive that I could not find my way to any of the spots that provided meals. A line started forming as soon as we pulled up for the first delivery. There were around thirty to forty people. They were very polite, or, at least, they were quiet throughout the prayer. One by one, they came through the line getting their bag and a drink. They would jump to the back of the line to try to get another. We had more stops to make so we told them couldn't give away the extras just yet. They would then start making all kinds of excuses: "I need one for my brother. He can't walk." Some were true, but most, I'm sure, were not.

After we were done, we drove a couple miles down the road to do it all again. I saw some of the same people at this place. A few of them had bikes and knew that they could get to the next stop if they hurried. I had never seen such desperation for a sandwich before. It was also interesting to me to see what the people did with their food. Most of the people would start eating their food right there, but some of them would walk away carrying it in their hand.

Lindsey, a girl who worked at City of Refuge, took me for a ride while she ran some errands. She showed me all around Atlanta: from Buckhead to Bankhead and downtown through midtown. Everywhere was so unfamiliar. I knew nothing about Atlanta. Truthfully, it was overwhelming. I was searching for places to sleep and people to meet, but it was a lost cause since I was just riding around in a car. I did not know where to start, but I did learn where not to go. Although the people at City of Refuge work with the homeless, they don't know the best places to go to actually be homeless; I had to learn that the hard way later on.

Lindsey advised me to talk to Charles for tips. Charles was a man who sat on the side of the road under a bride a couple miles from City of Refuge. He just sits there and looks at the cars that are stopped at the light. We rode by to see if he was there while we were out, and I spotted him. He appeared to be in his fifties or sixties. He looked worn out and tired. Lindsey prepared a meal for him about once a week and would take it to him.

I decided that Charles might be able to help me. I needed to know where to go and how to get food. The next day (Thursday), I fixed a sandwich and a Gatorade to take to Charles. I walked there alone. I was already starting to smell because I hadn't taken a shower in a few days. If I was going to tell him I was homeless, I needed to play the part.

On the way over to the bridge, I was offered drugs. I refused, but the man insisted that he had the good stuff. Oh, in that case . . . no, thanks. I kind of laughed a little bit. Did I appear that I needed a hit? I thought to myself that this was going to be a crazy summer for sure.

I finally got to the bridge where Charles was supposed to be and, sure enough, there he was. He was sitting down eating the last of his fried chicken. He looked at me as I walked up, and I asked if he wanted the sandwich and drink. He shook his head yes and took them, but he set them on the ground next to him. I wanted the drink for myself because the walk there was a little longer than I thought and I was very hot and tired. But, of course, I didn't ask for it back. I sat next to him, but he still didn't say a word. I wasn't really sure how to start talking. When in doubt, there are two options: (1) get straight to the point or (2) talk about the weather. I figured that he wasn't into the weather too much, so I told him that I was homeless and it was my first day on the streets. I asked him where the best place for me to go was. He mumbled something about getting a job and getting off the street. His advice was good, but it didn't help me very much. I asked him where he stayed, and he made it clear to me that he did not stay on the streets, although he had before. All he said was that he had a small place that way, as he motioned to the right. He works a little bit whenever the people that employ him are in need.

To this day, I don't know why he sits under the bridge for most of the day. He only looked at me as I walked up to him but not once while I was talking to him. After a short moment of silence, he got up and walked off. I guess he was finished looking at cars. I didn't learn what I wanted to, but I thought it was strange that Charles had a home. I also got a glimpse of how slow paced my life would be on the streets. I would have all day to talk with people.

When I returned to City of Refuge, Seth told me that Bethany (my friend's niece) had stopped by looking for me. I used Seth's phone to call her. I kept a long list of names and numbers in the back of my journal in case of emergency. She asked me if I wanted to make grilled cheese sandwiches with her on the streets. I didn't really understand how that worked, but what else was I going to do? She told me that she would pick me up around 8:00 that evening. That would be my first night out after dark.

Bethany pulled up into the driveway in her 1980-something Volvo. She had a bandana around her head and refused to shake my hand. She welcomed me with a hug. I got in her car and we went to the grocery store to pick up the bread, cheese, butter, and tomato soup.

We went to the place where Bethany serves sandwiches every week. I was still unsure of how this was going to work. We sat on the side of a little street in gravel and weeds with broken glass all around. It was right outside a tire shop that sat between a crack house and a hotel where prostitutes were known to hang around. There was a gas station right across the street that closed down not long before. It was dark and looked pretty sketchy. Bethany got her camping gear out and began to make a grilled cheese sandwich. The small mess kit she used reminded me of my Boy Scout days, except hers was much cleaner. We were the only ones there for a little while. This was also my supper though, so I was okay with eating one of the first sandwiches. We could only make one at a time because the mess kit was so small. My first thought was that Bethany should get a bigger grill in order to serve more people. In my mind, that would have been more economical, but the idea was to make the people wait so that we would have more time to talk with them. To see people waiting while we were making one at a time was frustrating to me at first, but I learned to sit back and enjoy their company. It was hard to get that through my fast-paced American mentality. With nowhere to be, I still felt like I had to rush. It takes a whole lot to slow people down in our culture.

Slowly, people would come by and ask us what we were doing. It did look a little strange, I guess. One young couple called it a picnic and thought that it was neat. They said that they would come back later, but they never did. After three hours that night, we saw eight or ten people. The kind of people that we fed ranged from drug users and prostitutes to the owner of the tire shop. He was there just about every week toward the end of the night.

While I sat there with all kinds of people, listening to all kinds of stories, God started to change my heart. I started to love these people. Serving people without feeling rushed taught me to truly see people—to see their pain and their joy. To look in their eyes and not think about what I was going to do next began to change me; and, hopefully, they could see that. At first I was a little uncomfortable talking with them because, to tell you the truth, I didn't really care. I had enough to think about, why would I care about some story that a guy I just met is telling me? I was still busy thinking about what I was going to do next. That proved to me just how much I cared (or didn't care, rather). True compassion comes once we come to a place where we can be still and acknowledge God (Psalm 46:10). It puts things in perspective. The next day, as I reflected on that night, I wrote these words in my journal: "Do not merely minister to people because you feel bad for not doing it, for you would be in danger of skipping out on blessing others and feeling God's joy. Love, provide meals, remember names, and truly care for others." This is a part of ministry that is often overlooked.

Chapter 3

First Night with No Roof

Day 6

It was Friday, June 6, and I planned to leave City of Refuge after five full days of spending time with others and learning everything I could about being homeless. I was planning on coming back Sunday to let everyone know I was okay. Seth was gone for the weekend, and I had no key. I guess this was like a trial run. Lindsey took me around town that morning. The plan was for her to drop me off while in town. The next moment was the first of many moments that I would dread.

Lindsey stopped the car and said, "Well I guess this spot would be as good as any." I thought to myself, "No, this is not good. Can't we just ride around for a while longer?" I cannot put into words just how much I did not want to get out of that car. It wasn't because the place looked dangerous, even though it did. It was hard because I did not know anything about where I would go from there or what I would do from then on; the feeling of not knowing where to even start looking for food or a place to sleep was miserable. I was already feeling empty and meaningless. I stepped out regardless of my hesitancy and grabbed my pack. Just like that, she was gone.

I sat outside for thirty minutes or so, and in that short time, I began to feel like I was nobody. I felt invisible. I had no purpose. I had nobody depending on me to do anything. Even though I knew why I was on the streets and that it was temporary, I still felt those emotions. Although many people were thinking of and praying for me, I felt like no one cared about me anymore. I had never felt so alone until that moment. My body trembled thinking about it. If I felt that bad then, how much worse was it for others who lived this way all the time?

I watched people make drug deals. I smelled the fragrance of marijuana (which became very familiar). I saw a lady feeding the pigeons crumbs from her sandwich. When she was finished with the sandwich, she gave about a fourth of it to the birds. I wondered if I should go in for the steal. I used to think that I was an independent person, but those first few hours on the streets made me realize just how much I depend on others and also how much I desired for others to depend on me. In Genesis 2:18, God said that it is not good for man to be alone. I concur.

I used a couple dollars that I packed to ride the MARTA (Metropolitan Atlanta Rapid Transit Authority) train. I didn't know where to go, so I rode the MARTA for about five hours. The train line is in the shape of a plus sign. I rode it in each direction a couple of times before I decided to get off. I used those five hours to read. I read through parts of the New Testament and was convicted personally and for the Church as a whole. I was trying to figure out how people who call themselves Christians act nothing like the saints I was reading about in the Bible. I asked myself, where are the works of the Christians? Works do not provide salvation, but they do prove salvation. Then I asked myself, where are my works? Is it possible to physically be where God has called you but still be out of His will? He was telling me to do what I was there to do; be homeless, not simply one who rides the train for hours.

The five hours on the train also gave me some time to think about where to sleep for the night. After looking at a map of the city, I decided to go to the largest park that I could find. It was a few miles north of downtown, where I started out. I started walking in the direction of the park, but it seemed so far away. That was okay though, because I didn't even know what I was going to do once I got there. It was hot and I didn't know exactly where I was going. I still felt highly uncomfortable, but this part of town did appear to be a lot nicer. Little did I know that in my state, nicer did not mean better.

I eventually got to Piedmont Park a couple hours before sundown. I had no clue if I would be safe here or not. I worried about the people that would walk by me during the night, but my main concern was the police. I heard stories from some of the people at City of Refuge about how homeless people would get put in jail for sleeping in parks. I did not want to go to jail! I guess that should go without saying, but then again, not many people want to go and live on the streets either. I was more terrified that I would be kicked out of the park than I was about being harmed by anyone.

I saw nicely dressed people walking in the park. I saw people riding their bikes and walking their dogs. I thought to myself, this was not the place for me. Then I found a bit of hope. I saw a very dirty man sleeping under a nearby tree. I felt comfort in seeing the homeless man there because I knew I would either not be in trouble for being there or not be alone if it was not allowed. It was strange to feel more at home when being around people with no home.

I didn't go over to talk to the man, but I did feel a lot more comfortable setting up camp on the ground nearby. I laid my head on my backpack and took my shoes off. I was still on edge though. I would see the guards drive by on their golf carts and hope that they did not spot me. I read a book to try to ease the feeling that I had. I was not very successful. It was getting dark, and I had so many thoughts racing through my mind. Do I need to hide, or do I need to stay in the open when I sleep? I had no clue what to do, and I was beginning to freak out. This was by far the most difficult and terrifying thing that I had ever done. I felt so weak in every way a person could feel weak. But just as I had almost had enough of doing nothing, I met my first homeless friend, Larry.

I was lying in a field under a tree when I noticed a middle-aged man walking toward me. He was not very clean, but he did not appear to be homeless. "Yo bro, you got a cigarette?" Larry asked with a strange Northern accent. "Nope, I don't smoke," I said. He sat beside me, "You homeless?" I kind of laughed to myself and said, "Yeah." He replied, "Me too." I was thanking God for someone to talk to and hoped Larry could help me out.

I told him that was my first night on the streets and that I was wondering where I could sleep at night. Larry had been staying there in the park for a few weeks. He said that this was one of the only parks that would allow homeless people to sleep there, as long as they didn't cause any trouble. What a relief! That was music to my ears! He told me that he just got out of jail a few weeks before and had nowhere to go. He didn't want to stay with his family because he didn't want to be a burden. He was waiting on his disability to go through so he could get his feet on the ground again. We even talked about the Bible for a while, and Larry explained that God was working in his life. I wasn't sure what to think, but his Bible was one of the only things he carried on him, which says a lot. Larry seemed pretty sane to me so far. I had not yet met anyone else to compare him with, but I was glad he was around.

Larry was homeless, but he tried not to act homeless. He wanted to go to a store and buy a soda, so we put what money we had together and walked to the store so that we could each get a drink. Whenever he had any money, he spent it, which is a huge contributing factor to his homelessness. That was something I became familiar with while on the street. When we returned, we picked out a good spot to sleep and lay down for the night. He said that it's safer to stay in the open. Besides, you can't really hide in downtown Atlanta. There are people everywhere at all hours of the night, and I didn't have much of a choice but to trust he knew what he was doing.

I rolled out my sleeping bag and gave him the jacket that I brought for warmth. I had been camping before, but nothing like this. To say that it was humbling is an understatement. It was one thing to walk the streets, but to lie down so boldly said to others, "Hey, look, I'm homeless." At this point, I could not care less if what I was doing was considered cool in some circles or even radical. I just knew this was a comfort zone that I have never been close to before.

We tried going to sleep around 9:00 that night. I'm not sure that I slept at all, though. I didn't even know if I could trust Larry, much less anyone else that would be out there. Speaking of people being out there, it didn't matter what time of night it was: people were out and walking around. These people, unlike the well-dressed joggers and people walking their dogs in the daytime, did not look very pleasant. When the sun goes down over Piedmont Park, it is a very different place. People walked right next to me cursing and making fun. Every step that I heard sounded as if it were headed straight for me. I'm sure that most of that was paranoia, but some people stepped right next to me, which I got used to.

Finally, the sun came up. Have you ever been camping before and been so cold or hot that you can't wait to get up, even though you were exhausted? That was how I felt. Six o'clock never came so late. I was waiting all night to see the sunrise just so I could be out of the misery that I was in. After the sun came up, we moved to the shade to get some more sleep. Well, I can't really say "more" sleep, but I think I did sleep a little because I was less afraid in the daylight. I woke up and saw just how many homeless people there actually were in the park. We were under trees and on benches, in the fields and on the stairs. I woke up sweating because the shade was gone. It was time to get up for the day and get busy doing whatever it is homeless people do.

Larry told me that we needed to start looking for somewhere to eat. I agreed because I was already hungry, and what else was I going to do? It was around 9:30 when we started asking his other homeless friends where to go. His friends told us that Ted serves food in about an hour. Ted was the man in charge of feeding the homeless people at a Catholic church downtown, and he was known for his amazing soup. Larry explained to me that I could get as much as I wanted. I couldn't wait, but we had around a four mile walk before I could taste Ted's delicious soup. What Larry's friends did next confused me. They understood that we had a nice walk ahead of us, so they offered to give us a bag of chips to hold us over. I thought that a homeless person would hold on to every bite of food he or she could, but this act began to show me how the homeless community looks out for each other.

I carried my hiking pack with me for a while, but Larry kept on telling me to stash it somewhere because we were going to be walking a lot. I was very suspicious of his intentions though. Would he try to ditch me and steal what little I had? Halfway there I couldn't take it anymore. I ended up hiding my pack under some leaves on Georgia Tech's campus. I started wondering if that pack was too much for the summer because of all the walking I had in my near future.

We got to the church just in time. We had to run the last bit of the way just to get there before they closed the doors. Larry was a little ahead of me, so I went in behind him. One of the volunteers at the doors asked me if I was there to volunteer. I was hot, hungry, and very tired. "No, dude, I'm here to eat!" I said. I guess I didn't quite fit in yet. Maybe I did not look worn enough, but that would come with time.

Ted's soup was amazing! We sat down in the basement with around seventy other homeless people while others served us. I was actually impressed. Before I came out here, I wondered just how much the churches would care for me. The volunteers kept asking me if they could get me any more soup or tea. I stuffed myself because I did not know when I was going to eat again, and Larry didn't give an itinerary. They gave me a pastry on the way out, and Larry and I started our slow walk back to the park.

By the time we got back to the park, it was around 3:00 p.m. I didn't have a watch, but I learned to ask people the time. I was still very hot and tired, but I was no longer hungry. That afternoon I met more homeless people. I had met homeless people before but never like this. This time, I was in their shoes. They acted very differently this time around. They seemed a little calmer, and they were real with me. There was no show being put on in order to get something out of me, which allowed me to see them for who they were. They had names, faces, and personalities that I was able to get along with for the most part.

I met two guys named Tony and Arthur. These guys did not stay on the scene long though. Larry and I were sitting on park bench with them. They asked how I got there when they found out it was my first few days out on the streets. The only thing I said was, "I don't have a room at my folks," which was technically true. Larry said, "Oh, it's that hard love kind of thing." I just shook my head, and they never asked any more questions. They both had a beer and maybe even some marijuana. I asked what they did, which is a strange question to ask a homeless man, but they must do something, right? The very short and edited version of what Tony told me was that he was a male prostitute. He explained that this area was great for that kind of business. He made enough money to get clothes and stay clean to get by on the streets, which was a foreign concept to me. He said that it was nice because he got to go into peoples' homes and take a shower and freshen up. I tried hard not to wear what I was thinking on my face. As if I wasn't already uncomfortable, it got worse. "You could make a ton of money doing what I do," he said. I was even more shocked. I said, "No thanks," which was a huge understatement, and thankfully the conversation changed.

After a few minutes of talking, Tony got into it with Arthur over something stupid and decided that he was going to beat Arthur with a piece of rebar, so I decided it was time to leave. This gives a picture of life on the streets and the fact that I would not be as bored as I thought. I later found out that the cops came by and took one of them to jail before it got too ugly.

I left Larry and walked around the park and sat next to the pond. This would normally be a nice relaxing place to be, but at the time,

I just wanted to be anywhere but there. Although I had met some people, I questioned what I was doing. Once again, I was more miserable than the day before. I did not want to read or write. I did not want to lie down. I did not want to sit up. It was impossible to feel comfort in any way, physical or emotional. The worst part was not that I was uncomfortable but the fact that I had no way to make it any better. I didn't even feel like praying. I felt like crying, but had nothing to give emotionally. I felt again that my life had no purpose, which was strange because I wasn't even a legit homeless man. I was on the verge of losing it, and it was only the second day. Any more of this, and I would start to lose my mind. Sanity is extremely hard to hold on to out there. I would even say it is near impossible for an extended length of time.

I tried doing anything to feel comfort. I went to the public bathroom at the park, hoping to cool off in the sink water. After that, I sat down and forced myself to start reading when Donnie came up. Donnie had short dreadlocks and looked like he came out of the Caribbean. He sat near me and asked, with his very deep and very slow voice, "What are you reading?" I did not feel like talking to anyone, but I told him. When I told him, he said, "Sounds deep." Then the conversation took off! He explained to me, while drinking his beer and smoking his cigarette, that he was homeless because all material things were going to pass away and he did not feel the need to own anything. Having nothing is a bit extreme, but maybe more people should have Donnie's mentality. He went on to tell me about the aliens that he saw and showed me his drawings of them. By this point, I was a bit fascinated at his stories and with nowhere to go, I just stuck around. We talked about the Bible, God, and other religious topics. We talked for about three hours, and it was in that moment that I knew why I was there, which gave me the motivation that I needed to keep going. Donnie did not come to know Christ that day, but I had a purpose. Donnie was a very strange character, but he was exactly what I needed at exactly the right time.

There was a large religious parade going on in the park right next to us while we were talking. It was a traditional Eastern religion.

There were large floats everywhere and people chanting. It was interesting to watch, but even more interesting was Donnie's response when someone came up to witness to us. You have to picture what was going on to understand the humor in it. There I was, a 135-pound dirty white guy, with a tall black man, and up comes a guy from India talking so fast that I could not understand him. About thirty seconds into his spiel, Donnie interrupts, "Wow, wow, slow . . . slow down. Dude . . . I can't understand anything you're saying. If you want to get across to people, you have to slow down." Donnie ended up taking one of the tracts that the guy had before the man walked away.

Larry joined Donnie and me under the tree after an hour or so. He knew that he would be hungry if he did not eat anything. He saw a few guys he knew walking by and asked if they had any food. Much to my surprise, they did. We followed them to the back side of the park where there were about fifteen people around a gazebo listening to a boom box and eating. I saw guys kissing other guys and all types of dancing. In the midst of seeing this ugly, sinful world in a way that I have never seen before, I loved these people because I was given the ability to see them as people and not beggars. They had no mask. These are the ones who fed us our supper that night. They had a whole chicken from Walmart and a bag of rolls. They had both been eaten off of by the time we got there, but I ate what was left. They freely gave it to me, and they didn't even know me. This was a community of people who accept and look out for each other in a way that I have never seen before. They had nothing to hide from me because I was one of them. That perspective was impossible to achieve any other way. Here is a note from my journal at the time: "Living in the park for just two days has been the hardest, scariest, but most beautiful thing I've seen." They were not into the politics of life or worried about their social status; they lived a simple lifestyle and took care of others in need. Should we become homeless for the sake of simplicity? No, but I definitely learned a lot about community that day. James 2:1 tells us, "My brethren, do not hold your faith in our glorious Lord Jesus Christ with an attitude of personal favoritism."

By that point, I wasn't sure if God had a partner to go with me or not, but it was not looking good. I survived with the people God gave me out there for two days. Actually, it was amazing that Larry was the first guy that I met because he was the sanest one I had met so far. He said that he believes that God sent me to him because he needed someone to talk with. I know that God sent him to me for the same reason. I was okay with doing this alone, but I still had a little hope that somehow I would meet someone who would go with me.

We went to sleep soon after the sun went down. I did not sleep any better, though. I think a spider bit my lip during the night because I woke up and it was swollen. Between the bugs and the people cursing at us, I could not sleep. Again, I waited intently on the sun to rise because I was planning on returning to City of Refuge in the morning. The name was much more fitting this time around.

Chapter 4

It's Better to Have Less

When a person follows God like they should, it will be anything but easy. It will be extremely tiring; but just in the nick of time, God will give rest.

Day 7

As soon as I could see the sun peek over the Atlanta skyline, I jumped up ready to hit the road. I packed my bag and left Larry a note telling him where I went. He was still lying on my jacket, so I just left it. It was a Gap jacket that I secretly inherited from my brother over the years, and it was the first of my few items to go. I knew that it was early, but I remembered Seth saying that City of Refuge served breakfast on Sunday mornings. I didn't know where they served, but if I got to the City of Refuge before they left, then maybe I could get there in time to get some food.

I took the MARTA, but it still took me a couple of hours to walk to the City of Refuge from the train stop. When I got off the train, I was in a dark, empty underground station. Another homeless man came up and asked me for some change so that he could ride the train. I didn't think that he really wanted money to ride the train, but I gave him some change anyway. This guy seemed spooky, especially in a dark train station, but I was probably starting to look spooky myself. After giving him the change, he dug through the trash can and grabbed something out of it and started eating it without hesitation. He told me how good it was as he passed by me.

If I was hungry enough, I guessed I would have the guts to do the same thing.

I got there early, but not early enough. I missed breakfast, but some people were still in the kitchen cleaning up. They didn't know me, but they let me use the bathroom and sit in the warehouse where they held services until everyone got there.

I had been out for two days, and I was already so nasty and sweaty from the walk; plus I had a swollen lip. As each minute passed, I felt more homeless and worn. I took my shirt in the bathroom and cleaned myself as much as I could, but it seemed to be pointless because I had to put on the same sweaty shirt that I was wearing before. I took off my already worn Georgia Bulldog hat and splashed cold, refreshing water on my face and head. I looked at myself in the mirror, watching the water drip through my short beard and wondering if I could do this. Maybe I learned what I needed after only two days.

Could I go back out there into a world I never knew existed? Of course I could see this world from afar, but to live in it for just two days opened my eyes to things I could not have imagined. It was like two different worlds. I felt detached from the world I used to live in, and I knew that people wouldn't understand me. I hadn't exactly warmed up to this new world of no responsibilities and no home yet, and I wondered if I ever would. By this point, I was stuck in the middle. I was adjusting to the homeless lifestyle and did not quite fit in yet, but regular people didn't understand me either.

As I sat down in the warehouse and people that I knew started showing up, I felt that I could rest and let my guard down solely because I was in the presence of people who cared about me. The body of Christ is so very essential to believers. It is extremely dangerous to be separated from Christ's body for any length of time. "And let us consider how we may spur one another on toward love and good deeds, not giving up meeting together, as some are in the habit of doing, but encouraging one another and all the more as you see the Day approaching" (Hebrews 10:24–25). So why was I going through with this? One person said that I couldn't help others if we were in the same position, but my intentions were not to help the homeless people around me at that time. My intentions were to obey God, and I could feel His presence giving me the power to do this and hang on to my sanity when it would have otherwise been impossible. Thank God: He is always right and I do not have to question Him. "As for God, His way is blameless; the word of the Lord is tested; He is a shield to all who take refuge in Him" (2 Samuel 22:31).

By this point, I figured that I was in it alone. I had no one else that was in likeness of mind to join me, which came as no huge surprise. Strangely, this was God's plan, and I would learn why later on. Since I did not have a partner to stay with me, and the body of Christ is essential, God placed people in my life to keep me going. The people at City of Refuge were so good in that area; just to be in their presence was uplifting. While the City of Refuge was helpful, it was far away from my new home, and I would soon have no money for train rides, so I also planned to go to church once a week. The college group met on Monday nights at Buckhead Church. I was not sure if I was going to tell them about what I was doing, but I knew it would be healthy to be around them.

I knew that I needed to lose my gigantic backpack because it was getting miserable to carry around in the heat. Keep in mind that a homeless people must carry everything they own with them everywhere they go. The least amount of things one can get by on, the better. It doesn't matter if that means you have to make do without a blanket. I had to weigh my odds. Would it be better to carry a sleeping bag around literally everywhere or make do without? That is why some homeless people turn down offerings. Bigger is not always better as a homeless person. You would think that the homeless would want anything they could get, but the reality is that if someone tries to give them a shirt or anything, the one they're wearing goes in the trash. All this to say: I brought way too much stuff.

Brad, a City of Refuge worker, and his wife, Jessie, let me know to ask if I needed anything at all. So I asked if they had a smaller backpack. They brought me one that day! It was perfect for what I needed. It was a small black backpack just big enough to keep the essentials in, like toothpaste, a journal, my Bible, and a little more room for a pair of shorts and maybe some leftover food. I left my old pack there with my sleeping bag, which was donated to someone there; a few books; and all my odds and ends (duct tape, pens, towels, etc.). I felt more prepared now that I had less stuff. That makes perfect sense, right?

Some people from the church that meets in the warehouse at City of Refuge gave me a few bucks, and the first thing that comes to my mind is that I will get to take my homeless friends out to eat. It reminded me of an orphan in Romania. He gave me his shirt only because I said that I liked it. As far as material possessions go, I had far more than him. Why was it so easy for him to give me his shirt then? I found myself holding on to things for the wrong reasons. I was saving the ten dollars in a slit on the sole of my flip flop for an emergency like a meal or a taxi ride to the hospital. How selfish of me.

After the church service, I went to the City of Refuge's guys' house and spent one last night under a roof. I was sitting on the couch when Larry's words came to mind: "I would love to be able to get a hotel room about once a month and just sit there and watch TV after a hot shower." I had the ability to do that at any time. It is a great understatement to say that I take so much for granted, even now.

God was teaching me how to be wise with my money (believe it or not), and He was teaching me that He is the one in control. If He says give (which He does more often than I do), then I have no right to question if I have the means to give. Giving should be at the top of a Christian's budget; the practice of giving shouldn't merely be reserved for the leftovers. It is impossible to give anything away faster than God can replenish, whether it be material, spiritual, or mental. Trust me; He will let you know when to give if you are truly willing.

Coming back for one day was God's way of giving me much needed rest. I'm not talking about mere physical rest but rather having a rest from people I didn't know I could trust. To see people working at City of Refuge and giving to others even when that means having to live a less comfortable life brought joy to my heart, which was no easy task at that time. Someone told me recently that absence makes the heart grow fonder. I think that people should sit back and enjoy the times when the body of Christ gathers because God intends it to be a delightful time. Please take my word for it; my desire is for your eyes to see what mine saw, without you having to do what I did. Even though it's not pleasant, going without for a season lets you know just how much you have. I'm talking about your loved ones in this instance—not a bed, or food, or a roof, but people who care about you.

Day 8

The next day, I made my way to the train station to head toward Buckhead to meet with college students for encouragement. Buckhead is the rich part of Atlanta. I don't remember taking a trip there and not seeing a Lamborghini or a Ferrari. You also won't see any homeless people on the corners. I'm sure they are around, but none were on display. Walking the streets is much different from being in a car. When I got off the train, I tried to find the church. It took me about an hour, but I finally made it about forty-five minutes before the service started.

I tried to keep from laughing because I looked so different from everyone there. I was sweating like crazy and had been wearing the same clothes for ten days straight, without a wash. I was in a place full of some of the most beautiful people I had ever seen. Honestly, the girls there could have been models. I was a little nervous but more excited than anything. There was a girl at the sign-in desk that asked me to fill out a card. I wondered what they were really thinking. She made regular conversation with me for a minute and then I asked where the water fountain was. That's what I really needed. I drank some water and splashed some on my dirty face in the bathroom and read a book until the service started.

When the service started, I stayed in the back of the dark room. There were a few hundred college students in the room while the band was playing. I was distracted by what people might be thinking about me. I knew that I smelled worse than my college roommate's shoes after baseball practice (which was pretty bad). I thought for sure that the people around me were hoping that I was not a person who raises their hands in praise for every song. I sat through the music and the message before we split up into small groups. I wasn't sure about the whole small group thing. I knew that I would be expected to talk, but what was I going to say? I didn't know if I should play it off and tell them some story or if I should tell them what I was doing. They had to have known that something was up.

So there I was, stuck in a room with about fifteen other people my age all telling each other what their lives were about. I didn't say anything until I had to. I was sharing a chair with an unlucky guy that got stuck next to me. I hogged the candy bucket, anxiously thinking of what to say. Nothing came to mind but the truth. I am not a good liar anyway, and this one would be hard to pull off. When it was my turn, I was so nervous that my voice was shaking, even though I told the truth. I failed miserably at remaining silent. By this point, the room was dead quiet and all eyes were fixed on me. I couldn't hold it in. I started by telling the people where I slept at night and then told them the reason I was living on the streets. I told the guy next to me why I stunk so badly and apologized. After I was done, the room remained silent for a few second. "I wondered what was going on," said one girl breaking the silence. All the other people started laughing and encouraged me in what I was doing. The questions would not stop: "How long have you been out there?"

"Where do you eat?" "Where do you sleep?" "Are you scared?" "Are you crazy?" I don't remember what the topic was that week because the majority of the discussion was about me living on the streets. I knew then that I had a weekly support group I could come to, which I needed after a week on the streets, and I was encouraged to keep on going.

Afterward, I was introduced to a group of guys who just finished filming a documentary on homeless people in downtown Atlanta called *My Concrete Mattress.* They were planning on showing the first preview in Dublin, Georgia, on July 11, where a few of them were from. It was about three hours from Atlanta. They wanted me to come with them for the debut. I asked if I could help in any way, but most of the things were already taken care of. They did ask if they could meet with me the next day and take me out to lunch so that we could talk more and gain insight on life on the streets. I gladly agreed.

After talking with the group, one of the girls asked how I was getting back. I told her either walking or the train. She gave me a ride back to my temporary home. (At least I could say I had a huge yard.) She dropped me off at one of the entrances to the park, said good-bye, and left. It was not easy stepping out of a car again but not nearly as bad as my first day out. Even though some of the people I just met lived minutes from the park, I felt as if I was stepping through a portal into another world far away from them. Watching her car leave was like seeing my old world disappear again. It was already night, so the "nice" looking people had already left. It was probably not safe to walk around there alone, but I desperately wanted to find Larry. I looked all over, but I couldn't find him. I just decided to lie down in the same place I had before. I was a little more scared this time because I was alone. I didn't have my sleeping bag either. It turned out to be one of the scariest nights of the summer.

I was a little cold and very uncomfortable after laying there in the open for a few hours. I wanted to see if Larry would come back to the same spot, but he never did. I tried to move to a different location to get some rest. I moved to a lighted area close to the water and curled up against a warm stone wall. I thought I was safe because of the light, but I was alone with no one in sight. There were other homeless people spread all over the park, but I could not see them. After an hour or so, I found that I was not alone at all! I kept hearing a noise, so I peeked out from under the bill of my hat to see what it was. I saw a man standing in the shadows staring at me. When he saw that I woke up, he motioned for me to come over there. "Over there" was a dark trail in the woods. I thought that he was offering me drugs like others had done, so I simply shook my head no and watched him disappear in the woods. I closed my eyes after twenty minutes but wasn't able to sleep because my heart was pounding. I tried to relax but was unsuccessful. The retention wall that I was getting my warmth from was only about four feet high. I woke back up to the same noise. "Psst! Psst!" Only this time, I saw that the light no longer provided safety. The man was standing on the wall about five feet from me! Looking back, I don't know how I remained as calm as I did. I hoped that I was dreaming, but this was really happening. For the sake of not being too vulgar, let's just say that this man showed me more of himself than I ever wanted to see. This got my full attention, but somehow, I took the hat off my face and stared at the man with a kind of dumbfounded look. He did not try to come at me, but I was getting ready to run if he did. I wanted to tell him off quite frankly, but I simply shook my head no once again. He shook his head too, in disappointment, I guess, and walked to the shadows where he stared for another few minutes. I never took my eyes off of him, and as soon as he left, I jumped up to move. I couldn't believe what had happened. All I wanted was a full night's sleep—it didn't even have to be a good night's sleep—but I didn't get any rest that night. I spent a lot of time praying for safety.

I ended up lying down next to a paved pathway until the sun came up. It was a beautiful sight to see "regular" people out early running and walking their dogs. I felt safe when they arrived but also humiliated because I was no longer one of them. It was so nice to have Larry sharing the humility with me before. To be alone made me want to bury my head in the ground and go to sleep hoping to wake up away from harm and shame. But the reality was that I was so tired that I couldn't find the energy to do much about it. I was so uncomfortable, hot, and hungry that I couldn't even sleep in the day when it was safe.

Day 9

I had seen a man with long hair riding his bike around the park for the last couple days. I thought that he was homeless, but I wasn't sure. He appeared to be middle-aged and seemed to be fairly happy. When I saw him in the park I went over to talk to him, but he was a bit short with me, so the conversation didn't last long. I later saw him eating in the same places that I did. He was always alone, but he took care of himself. It was like he knew that he was homeless, but he was going to make the best of it while he was there. His shirt was always tucked in, and the basket on his bike was always organized. He was the type of guy that might have a mattress to sleep on somewhere out here. He acted as if he didn't need anything from anybody. I wish that everyone out here thought like that, but a lot of homeless people act as if the world owes them for some reason.

I was hungry and only had a few bucks left. But without Larry's help, I had no clue where to go. I walked around and saw an Arby's. It was the first place that I saw, and I was tired of aimlessly walking around, so I stopped in. There was some kind of special, and I got three sandwiches for less than five dollars! While I was waiting on my food, a man walked in who appeared to be homeless. He was beaten and looked so worn out that he might collapse at any moment. The only thing that he carried was a large, dirty bag. He appeared to be in his sixties or so. The Arby's employees knew the man well and were kind to him because he doesn't cause any trouble. They chatted for a minute, and then he took a seat in the restaurant. He didn't have food, but one of the employees gave him a drink cup.

They gave me my food, and I went to find a seat. I didn't know if I should try to talk to this man or not. I started to walk by him to find my own place at a different table when he said, "Do you want to talk to me?" I said, "Excuse me?" He asked if I wanted to join him. He said that he felt that I wanted to talk to him. There are a lot of people out here that say a lot of things, and I don't know if he truly felt anything, but I was glad that he said something. He told me very early in the conversation that he saw goodness in me. Donnie (the guy that sees aliens) said the same thing. Maybe they could tell that there is definitely something different about me. It made me think: shouldn't most people know, somehow, that there is something different about me? It takes most people far too long to realize that about me, and it is my fault that they do not see Christ in me quickly.

This man's arm was in a sling and both of his eyes were not just bloodshot but pure red. I had never seen someone's eyes not showing any white before. His whole face was also swollen. I didn't want to ask what happened, but I was curious to know because I didn't want the same thing to happen to me while on the streets. He told me his story without me asking. Last night, he had two bags of groceries in his hands that he bought with food stamps. I don't know where he planned on keeping them, but he explained that it was nighttime. He also said that he was stubborn and should not have been. A few men told him to give them his groceries, but he refused. They broke his arm and beat his face before making off with his groceries. I didn't know what to believe and what not to believe out here, but it was clear that this man was in pain. Yes, he was obviously hurting physically, but there was more to it.

I gave him one of my sandwiches, and we talked for at least an hour. I told him my vague story about how I had no place to stay, and he gave me advice. He then told me that he had been living on the streets for more than thirty years. My heart was breaking so fast by this point. I just sat across from him and listened to his sad story. He didn't ever expect to get off of the streets. He even knew why he was out there and what it was that kept him there. He said that he was an alcoholic. Like I said before, the items that a homeless person carries are valuable, or else they would not have them. For me, it was a Bible and my journal, and for Larry, it was a Bible. But for this man, it was something very different. He started to smile as he opened it. He had about twelve different cardboard signs that he carried with him everywhere. I couldn't help but laugh a little bit. Here was a man that I would normally pass by while stopped at a light, and we were in Arby's having a conversation like two human beings. Go figure. "Wil wok four food," "im homles can I hav your chang?" He showed me each sign as if I were studying flash cards. He waited until the end to show me his best one though. "I aint gonna lie, I want som beer." He laughed as he told me that he got the most money from that one.

The employees at Arby's gave him some food from an order they messed up. He didn't eat it right then because he had already eaten what I gave him. He began to share how lonely he was and advised me to try to get off the street as soon as possible, which became very familiar advice. This was his life now. He had been there for so long that he wouldn't be comfortable with anything else. Huge tears rolled down his swollen face as he told me about how his family wanted nothing to do with him anymore. He knew that it was his own fault, and that is what upset him even more. He would pause every now and then and stare out the window to collect his thoughts. I could see his red eyes water when he thought of his life. By this point, I had tears rolling down my face as well, and not just because I felt bad for him. I actually didn't feel bad that he got beat up or that he has been on the streets for thirty years. I felt bad because his life was not how God intended and the things that he loved blinded him from the life that he could experience. In that moment, I saw the grace of God in my life. I had it better off than this guy even at my lowest point in life. God has given me so much. I honestly couldn't care less about having a bed, or a bathroom, or a big television at this point. I was most thankful that I had hope. Not hope in going back home in a few weeks, but hope that this world (on the streets or not) is not my home.

I had no clue what to say. I just wanted to know how I could help. I wish I had an amazing story about how God drastically changed his life from that moment on, but there was not much I could do. I showed him that I cared and I sat with him. Now, looking back on it, I believe that an hour of my time meant more to him than anything else. People that live on the streets of Atlanta know the Gospel message better than they know anything else. They hear it all the time. I just sat and listened until he was finished talking. He slipped his food to me and told me to put it in my bag so that the people that gave it to him wouldn't see what he did. For a man who owns nothing to do that says something that words cannot. After that, he simply got up and walked out, never to be seen by me again.

I was planning on meeting some of the guys I met at the church the previous night around 4:00 p.m. I had to figure out a way to call them without a cell phone, and most of the pay phones were broken. Arby's turned me down when I asked to use their phone, so I began my search for a working phone. I walked into a Barnes and Noble bookstore and asked if I could use the phone. She stared at me for a second with much hesitation. "Who you gonna call?" she asked. I told her that I was meeting some friends and that I didn't have a phone to call them with. I'm not so sure that I convinced her, but I was not going to lie. I wasn't going to tell her everything either, because surely she would have thought I was a lunatic. She finally handed me the phone and I called Eric (one of the guys from the church). He didn't answer. I was as polite as humanly possible to the lady because I knew that I might need to use the phone again. She may have seen how desperate I was because she let me keep using it. I eventually left a message on the phone and went to go sit down in the cool building to read and write, but I knew it would be only a matter of time before someone would make me leave. I felt very out of place in there. I felt like I should be outside and that I didn't deserve to sit on the nice chair in the air conditioned building, leaving behind my filth.

I waited in the chair for a little over an hour. By that point, I figured that I was not going to get a chance to see them until next week at church. I tried to call back every few minutes but got nothing. Time goes by so slowly when you're alone. After what seemed like a day, the lady at the desk came out and asked if I was Eli. I said I was, and she told me to come to the phone. Finally, I got a chance to talk to Eric. He told me to meet them outside in a few minutes, which gave me hope.

Two of them came to pick me up and took me to a restaurant right next to the park where I had been staying. I would have loved to go somewhere far from there, but it was food and from a restaurant! I couldn't complain. I sat with about six or seven guys and talked about life on the streets so far. I told them that I was miserable for the most part. They were all excited for me despite my demeanor. A couple of them said that they might stay out there with me one night! As much as I hoped they would actually do it, that night never came.

Eric wanted me to meet some of his friends who worked with homeless people downtown to get more advice. They drove me to a place called Safehouse, which is a place that feeds homeless people every night. I met some of the staff there and explained to them that I had been on the streets for a few days and that I was planning on staying there for a few weeks. By the end of the conversation, they knew the reason I was on the streets. Drew, one of the staff at Safehouse, looked at me and said that the only thing that he had to say was not to do it anymore. He was genuinely concerned with my mental state, which showed me that he had experience with homeless people. Others had been concerned for my safety, but Drew knew that my sanity was in greater danger than my health. I too did not know of the intensity of this danger until it swiftly came. Of course there are other dangers like death, but he did not mention anything about physical harm being done to me. Drew, of all people, knew the danger of being out there. Living on the streets for any length of time can very quickly mess a person up mentally. I told him that God was the only reason I was there and stressed that I was not doing this for any other reason. He said that he would pray for me, and that is all I wanted from him. He told me that Safehouse provides meals every night, but he was not there when the meals took place, so the staff there would think I was homeless just like everyone else.

Chapter 5

New Friends

After meeting Drew, the guys from church took me to meet John. John is a kind homeless man who volunteers at Safehouse. He is a little rough around the edges, but the guys thought that I should meet him. John was around thirty years old and had been in Atlanta for a few months. He came up after being released from a jail in Florida. John said that he was arrested for taking a sandwich from someone who offered it to him. The film that the guys from the church made featured John. John knew that I was new to the streets, but that was about all he knew. It was John who taught me how to survive on the streets, along with a few others. After introducing me to John, the guys left me at Safehouse to go to their homes.

I walked around the block for a while to try to get a little familiar with the area since it was going to be my new home. Instead of wide-open fields, like at the park, it was mostly sidewalks and skyscrapers. When it was time to eat, I went back to Safehouse to meet other homeless people and get some food. I couldn't find John anywhere, and the staff members had gone home for the day, so I began my search for new friends. I was back to feeling very alone. I was around two hundred other homeless people, but I only knew one of them, and I had not seen him yet.

Everyone was piling in the single door of the place to get a seat in the hot, smelly room. There was a stage in the room with band equipment on it. I thought that I was coming for the food, but they hold church there every night. Every night a different church fed people and ran the service. We were all packed in a room that could hardly hold us. I thought it must smell horrible, but it wasn't bad at all. Had I already become immune to the stench?

I was impressed by the music when it started. As a music major, I am not easily impressed by live music, especially in a place like this. Now I more fully understand the term "music to my ears." It was a glorious sound to me. It made me so happy during a difficult time. I could not help but stare at the musicians and smile with excitement.

When the music was over, a man started preaching. Before I go on, I want to mention something. The homeless people were there for one thing: food. If there was no food, then there would be no people. As I looked around the room, it was a very familiar sight. Of course the people appeared to be different, but their actions looked very similar to any church service that I had been to. There were some people standing and lifting their hands while singing and a few people sitting, but their attention was in the right place. But the majority wore a look on their face that said, "I am so bored, and I can't wait to get my food and leave." These people had a pretty good reason for coming to this church. If they did not sit through the service, they were not guaranteed a plate. Without a plate, they could not eat. Why do I go to church? Why do you go to church? Call me crazy, but if we all went to church for the right reasons, you know, like worshiping God for who He is, learning from God's Word, spending time with the body of Christ, serving and loving others, and so on, then why would pastors feel any sort of need to finish on time, or apologize for going over, or even joke about getting out on time. If God's Word is being preached, isn't that the reason we are there? In some ways, I looked up to these homeless people because everyone knew their intentions. They didn't go to church because it was the thing to do. There wasn't much hypocrisy in this place—that was certain.

Okay, on with the story. The man preached a sermon that soon became numbing to me. "God can bring you out of the place you are in. All you have to do is give your life to Him." There were encouraging Bible stories about God delivering people out of trials and tribulation. I was reminded day after day that I needed to get rid of all my sin. Preachers would tell us that we needed to quit drugs and alcohol and accept God and He would take care of us. There was an invitation almost every night for people to get saved. This sermon did not exactly pierce my heart, but honestly, I was a little bitter at the church at the time. This was my first church service where the church believed I was actually homeless. It spoke to someone, though, because a man went to the front and got saved.

Finally, I could eat! The line moved slowly, but sure enough, I got my meal on the way outside. It was a sandwich with a bag of chips, a bottle of water, and a Little Debbie snack for dessert. I finally found John outside and went over to talk to him because I was not sure where to go after dinner. He was in the parking lot with Mikey, another homeless guy I would become friends with. Mikey was wearing a clean, white, long-sleeved T-shirt that had a picture of animals and it said, "It's a zoo out here," advertising the Atlanta zoo. Mikey was twenty-six and had been here for only six weeks or so. Prior to Atlanta, Mikey was in jail in South Carolina for grand theft auto along with other drug charges. When he got out of jail, he had nothing and his mom and stepdad kicked him out of the house.

Mikey was a cool guy and very laid-back unless you got on his bad side. I had just met him and asked if I could chill with him and John, and he said, "Dude, yeah, you need each other out here. Welcome." There may have been a few F-bombs in there as well. I wondered why he had stitches on his face, but it didn't take me long to find out. That day was Mikey's first day out of the hospital, which is why his clothes were clean. Someone beat his head into the side of a building outside McDonald's on Peachtree Street downtown. Mikey dropped his two plastic bags with his belongings to fight, but the guy ran off. Mikey searched the area to find the guy, but he passed out on the sidewalk before he could find him. There was blood all over everything when the ambulance came to take him to Grady Hospital. He stayed there for a couple days before they let him out. Grady Hospital is free for homeless people, but you might have to wait awhile (unless you're unconscious). I hoped that I wouldn't have to visit the hospital, but I made sure I knew how to get to it just in case. I soon found out that all of Mikey's friends wanted to find the guy that did it to him. His incident was the topic of the night.

After eating and meeting in the parking lot, I followed John and Mikey to what they called "Crack Park," but I came to know it as the bathroom. Peachtree Street is the main street in downtown Atlanta and is full of homeless people. There were streetlights on all night, which was safe, so this place became my new home, and I never spent another night in Piedmont Park. The small park that we were in was next to a big bridge that overlooks I-75. I stared at the cars going by for a while, and imagined that I was among them, driving my car to go somewhere and now I was looking at the fast-paced world from the outside. I was removed from my previous life and now was a spectator of my old world. I was interrupted by two new people. The first was a guy who warned us not to stay in Crack Park because there are spiders that will bite you. He pulled his pants down and proudly showed us where a spider bit him on the butt. I just shook my head and questioned why I was there once again. Then I met Fred.

Mikey and John called him "Inbred Fred." Inbred Fred was a fictional character that Mikey made up to help him stay sane. It was just Mikey speaking in a strange voice about random things. After a few minutes, Mikey came back to join us. He says that if you don't play around and laugh a little, you will lose it, but I was thinking that he had already lost it by that point. In some strange way, he was right. He added the humor and fun, if you will, and John added the serious survival skills that I needed to keep going. These two guys became my partners even though they did not know what I was doing out there.

I didn't really know what we were doing in Crack Park, so I just followed them. When the sun started to go down, we headed to "the spot." The spot was John's idea of the best place to sleep as a homeless person in downtown Atlanta, no questions asked. My bed was now in the doorway of a church. The Catholic church faced Peachtree Street. I did not know how I was going to get any sleep on one of the busiest streets in Atlanta, but I didn't have much of a choice. We had to wait until it got dark because sometimes there were people still in the church, and the police would not let us get there early. If we were too late though, someone else would take the spot and we would have to settle for something less safe. Fortunately, that was not the case that night.

The doorway was about three feet deep and wide enough for the three of us to sleep there. That is all the protection that I had. Once again, there were people walking around all through the night right next to me, but at least I had some shelter. It was busier than the park. The lights shined in my eyes, and the cars driving by just a few feet from me created an uncomfortable but safe environment.

Day 10

If you ever have to choose between sleeping on concrete or grass, choose concrete! I would have never thought that concrete would sleep better than grass, but when there is nothing between you and the ground, concrete is the way to go. Grass is obviously softer, but the hard concrete is a small price to pay given the cons of grass. The grass gets itchy, cold, and wet from the dew. The ants and other bugs crawl all over you, making it nearly impossible to sleep. The concrete was warm from the sun, and there were no bugs. There was also no dew to get wet from. I was living in luxury, sort of. I did not sleep very much, but I did sleep better than I had on the streets so far.

We woke up really early to get away before the Ambassadors came to wake us up. The Ambassadors are usually nice, helpful people, but since I was in an unusual circumstance, their reputation was not as helpful. They are placed all over downtown to help visitors find their way around and to make it nearly impossible to sleep past 4:30 or 5:00 in the morning. I learned to dodge them because they did not care too much for us homeless people. I guess they were just doing their job, though. They looked quite humorous to me. They wore black pants with a white button-down shirt with badges on it. And the red and white safari-looking hats make them look like Crocodile Dundee wannabes. We were successful in waking up before they got to us that first morning.

After waking up, our first mission was eating. About one block from the church, a lady handed out a sack breakfast to homeless people. Her name is Mrs. Kay, and there is only one catch to getting a meal from her. You had to give her a big hug. For her to embrace around fifteen to twenty homeless people every morning was a light to me that shined in a very dark place. She said "God bless you" as she hugged me and handed me the meal. I grew to love the hug more than the meal as time went on, and I wanted the meal more than just about anything. There was love in her hug that I can't explain. Her hugs were genuine, and she did not hold back. She looked at me in the eye and did not appear to be in any type of rush. You could tell that she actually cared. I do not know much about Mrs. Kay, other than the fact that she worked downtown and gave a few minutes of her day to pass out breakfast to about fifteen homeless people before she started working.

Before she showed up, we all waited in line on the steps. That was where I met Josh, a nineteen-year-old who wore all black and never stopped talking about weed and sex. It was impossible to talk to him without hearing the F-word two or three times a sentence. I wish I was exaggerating. My patience was already thin from the street so it didn't take long to get annoyed, but I guess that's what I signed up for.

We went to Georgia State University's library after the crackers, pudding, and Vienna sausages from Mrs. Kay. All we needed was an ID to get into the library, and all three of us had one. I didn't have a pass to use the computer, but John did, so I just went to the back of the library and sat in a very soft chair and tried to keep from falling asleep. If I fell asleep, I would be kicked out and it would not be easy to get back in. John could only use the computer for one hour, so by the time he was done, Mikey and I decided to go find some lunch. John was going to work at Safehouse, so we split up. It takes a while to get around, so in order to eat, we had to walk for hours to get food, which makes it hard to get anything else done that one may need to do, like find a job or get an ID. Imagine taking a two- to three-hour trip for lunch and dinner, which is what it takes to feed yourself as a homeless person.

After walking for an hour, waiting in line for another hour, and listening to a preacher tell me that everything will be fine if I quit sinning, I get my stale baloney sandwich with a dry Danish pastry. I sat next to what I thought was a woman. I could not help but stare at her because I could have sworn that the stubble on her face was far too thick to be anything a woman could grow. She also came in on an electric wheelchair. How she charges it up, I do not know, because she had no home. I later found out that she is a he, and that he can walk. I guess it depends on the day of the week. These were my new neighbors and friends.

The previous week I made arrangements to meet Eric, one of the guys from Buckhead Church, down at Piedmont Park to stay on the street with me. I made my way to the park, but I was an hour too late. I figured that he didn't wait around, so I looked for Larry while I was there. I didn't find him, but I did find Donnie. He told me that Larry was looking for me. There is not much you can do in order to get in touch with people out there other than looking. It's sort of like this huge hide-and-seek game that lasts for weeks. I didn't find Larry that day, so I decided to head back to Safehouse.

Some people at City of Refuge gave me about five bucks, so I used the money for a train pass, but I didn't go straight to Safehouse. I couldn't bring myself to step off the train. I stayed on the train for a while and didn't want to see any more inner city. Even though I met some new friends, I still felt very alone and miserable. I didn't know what I needed to do. I even considered leaving and going home to keep my mind intact. I got off of the train at the northernmost station to see a little bit outside of downtown. I love the inner city, but I wanted to see something other than buildings. There were not very many people at this train station, which was nice. When I got off the train, I saw a pay phone with the handset still attached, so I decided to call home. It was my first time calling home since I had left City of Refuge. This may have also been my first time using a pay phone. I dialed collect and then followed the instructions to get in touch with my parents. I attempted to reach them twice, but I never got through. At this point, I couldn't even get out of this if I wanted to! I don't know what I would have said or if I would have told them to come get me, but I didn't even have the ability to talk to them. I prayed and asked God if I should leave or stay: He let me know that I would know when to leave, but it was not that day. "Give us this day our daily bread" (Matthew 6:11). God's grace was enough to get me to the next day.

I returned to Safehouse after my failed attempts at reaching my parents. I watched another band play and another preacher preach. The same man that raised his hand the night before to get saved raised his hand again when the invitation came. I felt like I was reliving the night before and that not much had changed. Afterward, I walked with Mikey to Underground Atlanta to look at the things that we could not buy. Underground is a tourist attraction with lots of little shops. The last time I was there, I was about eight, and the only thing I remembered was that I saw a man playing a saw for money. Come to think of it, he was probably just a homeless guy like me trying to survive. Mikey and I sat on the steps next to an empty fountain. The security guard quickly told us to leave. Mikey got an attitude with the guy, but it did no good, so we walked to reserve our sleeping spot for the night.

On the way to the spot, we walked right by the place where Lindsey dropped me off on that first night. That felt so long ago, and this time it felt more like home. When we got to the spot around 8:30, John met us and we just talked about the day. A well-dressed couple started to walk straight toward us, which was very unusual. Most well-dressed people try their best to look the other way and act as if they never saw us, but these people walked up to us and asked if we wanted their leftovers. I look at John and questioned if I should trust them, because he had more experience than I did with this sort of thing. We looked at them and said, "Oh, yeah!" then we said thanks and they gave us three heavy boxes and left. It looks as if they did not even touch the food. There was so much food in there we could have lived off of it for a few days if we had a fridge. I probably ate six cinnamon rolls that night. I was in heaven!

It rained that night, but I didn't get very wet because I curled up in a ball near the church door. I stared across the street at the bottom of the SunTrust skyscraper. It's a nice plaza area with stairs and an entrance halfway underground that would provide shelter for at least twenty people. I knew that if I went over there though, I would be caught by their security guard and possibly arrested, so I decided it was best to curl up and stay put in the doorway. I woke up more sore than I have ever been. I had to use my arms to pick up my aching legs in order to get up.

Day 11

Early the next morning, Mikey and I went to fill out a job application. A couple days before, a friend of Mikey's told us about a place that was hiring. All I knew was that it was custodian work for some show not far from where we were. I wanted Mikey to get a job, and so I decided to go with him to keep a low profile. I didn't want it to seem like I was consciously trying to stay on the streets. I figured that it might be another good experience, too.

The application process was just like normal. We made our way to a small office at the bottom of a skyscraper after walking through the loading docks. There were a couple of ladies working at the desk inside an unorganized office about the size of a walk-in closet. A couple of construction workers came in and out while we were there. I gave them my information on paper. I had no address or phone number to give them though, but I did have Mikey. Fortunately, he had a Facebook girlfriend with a phone number and an address that we could use for the job application as well, even though she lived in North Carolina and neither of us had personally met her. After finishing the application, we were told to come back in a few days to see if we got the job. I hoped that they would not call to let us know anything, but all we could do was show up when they told us to. The application process was painless, but actually getting the job was fascinating and you will see why.

After a restless night and filling out a job application, we made our way to Central Library about ten minutes away. Central is a four-story library just a few blocks from where I live, or rather sleep and eat. They didn't open until 9:00, so we had to wait awhile before we could go in. At the library, I would be able to use the computers for twenty minutes at a time, but I had to wait in line for about thirty minutes to get online. The library provided more than just computers, though. This was also where I could come and brush my teeth and try to freshen up. I was in the bathroom stall the first time I came to the library and overheard the security guard training a new guy: "Kick anybody out who brushes their teeth, shaves, or is bathing." That was a close call.

I usually went to the library with Mikey. He has a library card that allows him to use the computer for two hours at a time. While I waited on him, I would write in my journal and study scripture. It amazed me how fulfilling God's Word was and still is. It has the ability to fill me up every day so that I may pour out. I hate not having anything to give, so I had to spend time reading and in prayer so that my trip would not be in vain. "Blessed be the God and Father of our Lord Jesus Christ, the Father of mercies and God of all comfort, who comforts us in all our affliction so that we will be able to comfort those who are in any affliction with the comfort with which we ourselves are comforted by God" (2 Corinthians 1:4).

One of my main intentions in taking this whole trip was to learn to rely on God. I thought that I was doing pretty well to take the step of actually doing something like this, but God requires everything, not 50 percent, not 99 percent. I knew that I had a ten-dollar bill that I was holding on to just in case I didn't get a meal or two. That money could have fed me for a few days, but that put my trust in myself. It is like I was saying to God, "I trust you, but just in case, I'm going to hold on to this." God provides in many different ways, and sometimes He will give us things in very practical ways; but I knew that this was something that God wanted me to do and that I should not hang on to anything. God wants us to let Him take care of us, but we get in the way so many times by trying to take care of ourselves. It wasn't easy, even though it was just ten bucks, but my conviction was too strong. This is what I wrote in my journal: "I have learned to trust God with safety in the darkest times. When I sleep in dangerous places or walk through rough neighborhoods, I know that He is beside me. I don't have to wonder where my next meal is coming from though. That is why I am holding on to this money because I know I can eat if nothing else. It must go!"

While I was sitting in the library, I had time to think about everything that was actually happening. Reality would set in, and I'd realize that this was no dream and that I was now a homeless person. The first week was completely miserable, to say the least, but I was starting to get used to this life. I was starting to sleep better on the sidewalk and get used to walking hours every day to get food. I didn't know if that was good or not, but at least it made it a little easier.

I was waiting for Mikey to finish with the computer to let him know that I had ten dollars to spend. When Mikey came over to the table where I was, he asked what I wanted to do now that he was done at the library. I looked at him and had a huge grin on my face because I knew exactly what we were going to do. The day before, we saw a fudge shop in Underground Atlanta that looked so good! I said with a strange grin, "Want some fudge?" He said, "How? We gonna steal it?" I think he was serious. "Nope," I told him about how I had some money, and he started laughing and called me a couple of colorful names (in a joking voice). If a homeless person has any money at all, it is expected that they share it with their friends because saving money was not an option. It was like I had been holding out on Mikey.

We left the library and went straight to the fudge shop. We spent all the money that I had on different kinds of fudge. Ten dollars didn't get us very much, but what we did get was so delicious! I savored every bite. Mikey and I saved some for John as well.

Was wasting the money that I had on fudge wise? I think so. Holding on to what God wants us to get rid of is wrong. Easy, right? How many times have I known that God wanted me to get rid of something and I held on to it too long because I wanted to seek out the best way to get rid of it?

Later that night was grilled cheese night with Bethany. This was the first time that I walked to her house to meet her. I didn't realize that her house was about six miles away! I started walking early enough to get there before dark. It was nice and I would even say necessary to talk with Bethany because I told her everything, and I knew that she would understand where I was coming from.

Not long after we set up the camping stove, we had our first visitor. Fannie was her name. She was an older lady who sat down on the curb next to us. She ate one sandwich and just sat there for a while. Most of the time, people who are in need get what they need and leave, and the same was true with grilled cheese sandwiches, but not for Fannie. For her to stay was out of the norm from what I had seen thus far. I thought she might stay until she got hungry again. Every time I offered her water or tomato soup, she politely shook her head no. Fannie wore a pleasant smile on her face and spoke softly. When Bethany or I would ask her a question, she would answer it without expounding on anything. Before this journey, I would have thought that a lady just sitting in our company would be peculiar. I would have thought that she had mental issues and would wonder why she'd just sit there if she didn't want to talk. But I had to come to understand the feeling of loneliness from my short time on the streets. I do not know where Fannie came from or what she had to go back to, but she stayed there listening to us talk and watching us feed others for the whole time we were there. She sat there for two or three hours after she got some food. She would not take any with her either. Fannie was not there for the food. She was in need of much more than a grilled cheese sandwich. The look on her face and her actions told me that she wanted to be there. She didn't want to talk, and she didn't necessarily want us to talk to her. She needed to simply be in the presence of people. Maybe she felt peace there, but I don't know. Something kept her there. We must ask ourselves how many people like that are there in the world.

When I returned to the spot to meet Mikey and John, Mike walked up. Mike was in training to become a Catholic priest. He stays down the street from the church where we sleep. He was only there for a summer internship at the church. He had a bald head, and when he asked us questions, he looked at us in the eye until we responded. He did not interrupt us or condemn us. He cared about us, and I was not the only one to see his genuine concern.

Mike first asked us if he could refill our water bottles. We said sure. It is no fun going to bed hot, much less hot and thirsty—no fun at all. When he returned, he sat down with us. Don't take that lightly. It is a very humbling experience to sit down on the sidewalk with homeless people. For someone not on the streets to hand us food was amazing, but for someone to lower themselves and sit on the dirty ground with their nice clothes on was off the scales! It took humility for him to do such a thing because other people would also see him and probably mistake him for one of us. God forbid! I'm sure that John the Baptist was worried about his image, too. Worse than in the park, curling up in a doorway where lots of people saw me was so humbling that I cringed and actually took a deep swallow when I did it the first few times. I guess I was trying to hold on to a bit of my pride. Mike talked to us like we were people, unlike the majority of the preachers that I saw. He asked us about our lives, and yes, homeless people do have lives. It was amazing to see the care in him. He later went to his place and packed us what he had into three bags. He did not even have much, but he gave what he had: a jar of peanut butter that was half empty, some carrots, and some crackers. He went away for the night, but he said that he would see us later.

Day 12

The sound of car horns woke us up at 4:00 a.m. I usually sleep through them all night, but this one didn't stop. The long beep did not fade into the distance as usual. Before I could open my eyes, John woke me up and said that we had to get moving quickly! I looked up to see two Ambassadors in a jeep parked in front of the church. One of them was hanging out of the window yelling at us. "Where are you from? Why don't you stay there!" I was used to being mocked by this point, but not by someone who works for the city. First of all, I was pretty upset that it was 4:00 a.m. and I was awake, but this guy made me furious. Mikey was cursing at him, and I'm not so sure that I was far from doing the same, but the Ambassadors just laughed at us while yelling and honking the horn. This was a new low. I always found some way to be knocked down a notch or two.

The three of us were dead tired as we searched for a place to keep sleeping for a couple hours. It was hard to do because the Ambassadors looked everywhere for homeless people to mock. I think they did it to make downtown presentable for the business people and tourists. We found a place behind some animal statues near Crack Park. It is not the ideal place to sleep, but we were hidden from people trying to wake us up.

We woke up about an hour later and got breakfast and a hug from Mrs. Kay. There is a public bathroom that opened at 7:00 a.m. in Woodruff Park about six or seven blocks down from the church. We all headed there to take advantage of it. The bathroom was also a hang out spot in the morning for homeless folk, so we would meet up with some friends there sometimes. Being homeless does have its perks. If I met someone and wanted to hang out with them right then, I could. I had nothing to stop me from doing so: no job, no classes. If I wanted, I could spend a few days with them. That morning was something like that. I left the bathroom to hang out with Josh (the young guy who dresses in black). He led me to a library on the west side of town where I could get online for as long as I wanted. It was a long walk, but I wanted to update my blog to let my friends and family know that I was alive and what life was like.

I knew that I needed to get fuel (Bible time and prayer) while I was there as well, so I was looking forward to spending some time inside at a desk. I started off at a desk for a couple hours while I read and prayed and then moved to a computer for a few more hours. This is where I talked to some of my friends online.

After spending half a day at the library and skipping lunch, Josh and I decided to get to Safehouse for a meal and listen to another church service. Meeting two hundred friends for dinner every night was kind of neat. Sometimes a fight would break out and the cops would come, so it was never boring. Jesus shared meals with people all the time and I can see why: a meal brings all types of people together. I loved coming to see everyone at the end of every day. After the meal, the three of us (John, Mikey, and I) went to the spot for the night.

The spot had been taken, but there was still a little bit of hope. Right next to the doorway, the church building goes in about a foot, providing a little bit of shelter. We waited it out because sometimes people will move. We watched from across the street, out of view.

The man that was in the spot got up! A spark of hope! I watched him walk over to the next best spot, where we were about to lay our heads, and he started to pee right there. I couldn't believe it! "This is a load of hogwash," I said to John. He just laughed and replied, "Well, guess we better start looking for another place." We headed for the place behind the animal statues near Crack Park (not a place anyone wants to be at night). Within just a few minutes of being there, I was offered weed and someone else asked us if we had some crack. Later a guy sat next to Mikey and smoked some crack; hence the name, "Crack Park."

I woke up in the middle of the night to a familiar sight and sound. There was a dirty looking cross-dresser standing five feet from us and staring. "Not again," I said to myself. I was not nearly as scared this time because I had a few friends with me. He makes the same noise to get my attention: "Psst! Psst!" I am sure that he was looking for a partner for the night. I just shook my head when he motioned for me to come over there, and he finally walked away. This type of thing happened just about every night.

Day 13

I sat through around ten sermons a week. For the most part, it was the same one over and over again. My attention was fading faster and faster during the messages because it began to sound like a broken record. Around the corner from Safehouse, a church serves hot dogs in the evening once a week. After I got out of one service, I stood in line and listened to a gray-headed preacher telling me what I heard ten times that week already: "Jesus loves you and wants you to live for Him." Everything he said was true. "You can get your life straight tonight." His voice was amplified with a microphone and a small guitar amp powered with a converter. Okay, I'll be dead honest: I was starting to get a little annoyed and quite bored. I met some new people, and I was quietly talking to them in line. (By the way, the line does not start moving until after the preaching is done.) I was talking to some new friends when the preacher walked up to me and said through the mic, with a harsh tone and serious demeanor: "Son, you need to be quiet now. This is why we are here: to share God's Word." I wanted to tell him everything about me and about how he looked to all my friends (with love, of course), but I just got quiet instead.

Sometimes I feel that we try to squeeze the Gospel into ministry when it should obviously be the other way around. I thought that the Gospel was ministry. Nowadays, Christians often try to think of the next new thing to attract people. What kind of music do we need to get people here? Let's feed the homeless so they will stay and listen. How do we get people to come and sit through a message of the Gospel of Jesus? I have some ideas: What if we led a life that is holy and set apart? What if we did not allow things to enter our homes that shouldn't? What if the trials and afflictions of the world did not affect Christians the same way they affect nonbelievers? What if we treated others better than ourselves, loved our enemies, and stopped complaining? What if Christians looked different from non-Christians? I do not think that décor, food, and games at church are wrong—unless those are the means we use to attract people to God. God attracts people to God, and the means in which He graciously chooses to bring people to Him are his followers! I am not saying that we should stop feeding and preaching to the homeless, but I am saying that we should care for every aspect of their lives: body, mind, and soul. Look into their eyes and remember their names.

Day 14

Mikey wanted a shower and John needed some medicine for his feet. It was Saturday, June 14, and we had food left over from the night before. We needed to go to a Publix supermarket to get the medicine, and it would take up most of our day just walking from place to place. John was able to get a prescription from Grady Hospital that allowed him to get the medicine for free.

Gateway is a large resource center for homeless people. They have rehab programs, washing machines, and much more, but I was only going to use it for the shower. This was my first of three showers for the summer. I didn't know what to expect for my first shower, but I was ready for some fresh water. I had to walk in and wait in line for a small bar of soap that was broken in half and a ripped towel. I exchanged my ID for the soap and towel and went into the shower room. There was a small room with two sinks before I came to the showers, with two or three chairs to place my belongings on while I showered. This was again another low for me. I was humbled yet again. There were about ten shower heads on the wall with no stalls. There were about six other homeless guys all taking a shower, which left few shower heads to choose from. I took the shortest shower I have ever had. At least the water was hot, though.

When I was finished, I felt so refreshed until I put on my nasty clothes. It seemed pointless because my sleeveless shirt was still soaking wet with sweat. I brushed my teeth for about ten straight minutes while I had a sink that I could use without fear of being kicked out. I had some deodorant, but it's only good for about half a day out on the streets. I would apply it once, and then it was no use after that with the amount of sweating I did.

After the humbling shower experience, we started our two-and-a-half-hour walk to Publix, only to find out that the Publix we went to did not have a pharmacy. There goes the day. Five hours of it were spent walking, and we had nothing to show for it. This Publix was not far from the library on the west side of town, so we stopped by before heading to Safehouse.

Chapter 6

Rejuvenation with Believers

People often ask me what homeless people do all day. You now have a glimpse of what my typical day looked like, but I've broken it down to give you a better idea.

5:00–6:00 a.m.	—Wake up or get woken up.
6:00–7:00 a.m.	—Wait on the steps where Mrs. Kay works to get breakfast.
7:00–9:00 a.m.	—Walk to the bathroom and wait in the park for the library to open.
9:00–11:00 a.m.	—Read, write, and use the Internet in the library. Fill up water bottles and try to not get caught brushing my teeth.
11:00 a.m.–12:00 p.m.	—Walk to find food or skip lunch to look for a job and help friends get their IDs.
12:00–2:00 p.m.	—Wait outside in food line and then eat.
2:00–3:00 p.m.	—Walk back toward Safehouse.
3:00–5:00 p.m.	—Play cards in the park or go to the library.
5:00–8:00 p.m.	—Sit through the services at Safehouse and then eat.
8:00–9:00 p.m.	—Walk close to the spot and wait for it to get dark before we move in.

9:00–10:00 p.m.	—Sit in the spot and talk about the day.
10:00 p.m.–5:00 a.m.	—Try to sleep through the noisy streets of downtown Atlanta to wake up and do it all again.

As you can see, the majority of my time was spent waiting and walking to get food. I felt bad that I didn't have to beg for money yet because there were so many churches that fed me. I wanted to experience many aspects of homeless living, including begging. I didn't have to play my harmonica for money, although I probably wouldn't have earned much. The only thing I had learned to play was "Low Rider" by War. John and Mikey said it was good, but their optimism didn't push me enough to make money with my skills, or lack thereof. I felt that things were slowing down and that I wasn't humbled enough because I had not begged for money or eaten out of a trash can, but what God had shown me was how to love others and minister to their needs. At this point in my journey, God had also shown me a glimpse of the intensity of being alone and just how harmful and even dangerous it can be. We need each other.

Day 15

I asked Mikey and John if they wanted to go to church with me, but they declined. I walked to the evangelical Christian church across the street, where some of my friends sleep at night, and sat in the back row. I was twenty minutes early, but I had nothing else to do. I used to wonder why people rarely walked into a church if they did not know anybody. How hard could it be to come to church and meet people? But then I actually felt it. Yes, I had a beard and sleeveless T-shirt, I smelled horrible, and I felt out of place. I felt out of place because I didn't know anyone, not because of my homelessness. Two people spoke to me, and they both worked at the church.

Honestly, I didn't want to be there. Welcoming would not be the word that I would choose, but this was only the first try. I did find out through the announcements that first timers eat for free after the service! I was already hungry because Mrs. Kay didn't work on the weekends, so Sunday breakfast was usually skipped.

At the end of the service, I grabbed my bag and searched for the food. I asked someone where it was, and he pointed me in the right direction. I would smile at people in the hall and look at their reaction. Usually they would give me a short head nod and then look elsewhere.

I found the food! It seemed like I just needed to walk in, so I got in line. But then someone made it clear to me that I needed a ticket so that they could have a head count. I apologized and he gave me one. It was buffet style, and I piled the food on my plate. I found a table and sat down by myself. There were people everywhere, but no one sat with me. I felt very out of place again, and I really would have loved to talk to someone about anything at this point. I would have loved to talk about the weather or even the food. I just did not want to hear the F-word in every sentence. The guy who first spoke to me before the service asked me a few questions, but then he left after about a minute. I wanted to leave because I was so uncomfortable, but it was a buffet! Should I leave and go back across the street where I was comfortable, or should I just stick it out at the table by myself and enjoy the hot food? I could not pass up the food, so I stayed until I finished eating.

I was glad to get out of there because I felt too out of place. I was ready to get back to my comfort zone and return to the hot street again. The other lady that talked to me before the service saw me and stopped me on the sidewalk outside of the church. She asked some questions about where I was from and where I lived. I told her the same vague story. I did feel bad for keeping everything in, but I wanted to be treated like a homeless person. When I told her that I slept across the street, she offered for me to use the church to escape from the heat or other people. She actually cared! I was relieved to find someone who not only cared about me but also showed it.

Sadly, my expectations of churches were not so high coming out here, but she impressed me. People on the streets honestly know as much or more about God's Word than a lot of churchgoing people do. Some of them could preach better than the services I've seen out here. Homeless people do not need another sermon; they need Christians to listen to them with not only their ears but also their hearts, because that will spark action just as this lady did.

After I was back with John and Mikey, I stared at the nicely dressed church members piling out of the doors where I slept. I chuckled to myself as I wondered if they had any clue what goes on there every night. When I bragged about how good I ate to Mikey and John, they said, "I knew I should have gone to church with you." "Next time," I replied.

Compassion, love, and charity: those were the things God was teaching me. Of all the things that I thought I would learn—like appreciating my bed, food, and roof; trusting God with everything; and seeing how the church takes care of the poor—I didn't expect to come away learning how to love more. I thought that I already loved people. My human love can only go so far and it can only take so much.

If someone writes a love song that says things for the sake of being sweet even if they're not true, what would their partner think if they found out? My point is that if we as Christians minister for the wrong reasons, then we can very easily cause more harm than good. Do you minister to others because it looks good to other church members? Do you do it because you feel bad for not doing it? Do you serve because it is expected of you and others asked you to? Do you do it because the Bible says to and follow through out of obligation? Or do you do it because you have genuine love for serving that is truly out of this world?

I wish that there was no need for me to write this, but from what I've seen, the majority of the church members taking care of us were not serving from an outpouring of love. Jesus reminds the Pharisees on two separate occasions that He desires compassion more than sacrifice (Matthew 9:13; Matthew 12:7). Paul reiterates this many times: "And if I give all my possessions to feed the poor, and if I surrender my body to be burned, but do not have love, it profits me nothing" (1 Corinthians 13:3). Trust me, people know when it is genuine or not.

While we were walking to the water fountain, my friend Mikey told me that he feels blessed. His statement stopped me in my tracks. This guy literally has nothing. I asked him why he felt like he was blessed. "Dude, we can drink the water that we are given and eat the food without the fear of dying because of it. We have to walk to get our meals, but it's not always life or death like it is for others around the world. Eli, **we have it made**." I figured that it was not the best time to tell him that I had a car and that I was planning on going back to school in a few weeks. "Yeah Mikey, I guess we do."

That night I went to bed thirsty and hot. My mouth was dry, and I was lying on the hot sidewalk. Mikey's words ran through my head. "Eli, we have it made." I didn't feel like I had it made, but I knew that I could have walked a mile to get some water at a water fountain if I wanted. That doesn't seem very convenient to me, but this homeless guy recognized how much we did have. I went to bed thirsty that night, but I guess it wasn't that bad.

Day 16

The noise of car horns and sirens faded in and out. When the noise got louder, I decide to crack my eyes open. I quickly realized that I was outside under a big magnolia tree. What was I doing outside? My body was sore from sleeping on a concrete bench, and I had no shoes on. I sat up quickly to find out what in the world was going on and where in the world I was. Within a few seconds, it hit me: oh, yeah, for some reason I decided to be homeless for the summer. I was a little disappointed because I thought that I was dreaming, but my dream quickly turned into reality.

I have woken up from deep sleep before, staring at the ceiling and feeling confused because it was unfamiliar before realizing that I was away for vacation. This was one of those times. I honestly did not know where I was or what I was doing there for a few seconds. I remembered that I was on the way to the church in Buckhead. I knew that it was a long way, but this was my first time walking there. I took off for the walk before noon to make sure that I would get there by 7:00 p.m. Along the way, I stopped to take a nap in the shade of the huge magnolia trees in front of Piedmont Hospital. I must have slept better there than I thought I would. I woke up slightly disoriented but soon remembered that I had sat down to take a break in the shade. I wanted to hide because I didn't want to be kicked out, but I decided to lie down. Then the tennis shoes that were tightly tied to my feet came off. I woke up wondering where I was. I didn't know what time it was, but I figured that I should get going. I saved my sandwich from the night before so that I would have lunch on the way.

I spent many hours walking up to this point, and God began to show me more of the world that is often a blur when driving. I walked through some neighborhoods and on some main roads. It's one thing to take a wrong turn into a dead end while driving, but when walking, it meant another forty-five minutes, which happened a couple of times. Walking slowed my pace down a good bit, obviously, but it forced me to see what existed between point A and point B. By walking, I could see and smell every plant and breathe the somewhat fresh air. I could look at others walking their dogs or playing in the playground. I did have somewhere to be, but I had hours to get there. I used to move so fast that I didn't truly know what was going on around me. I fear that moving too fast physically often bleeds over to our mentality as a whole, which can harm ministry in many ways. For instance, when people were ministering to us, it often seemed that they could not wait to move on to what they had planned next. It is hard to show people you care when you rush through your conversations with them.

I finally made it! "Can I help you?" said the security guard at the church. "Maybe, what time is it?" She told me that I was a few hours early. Oops! I made better time than I thought. I figured that I could just wait around the church until it started. You know, sit in a room or even help get ready. I was sweating a lot by this point and out of water. I asked if I could talk to someone who was helping with tonight's meeting. She then called for them to come meet me.

Some of the college students knew me from last week, but the staff did not know anything about what I was doing. I could have used that to my advantage to test them, but I didn't feel that would be a wise move. Three people walked through the glass door to see me standing there all homeless looking. I told them everything in a timely manner. They stared at me with a look of confusion as if they had no clue what to do. I guess I expected them to respond with something other than "the church doesn't really open until an hour before the service." One of them did ask if a wanted a glass of water, though. I accepted and offered to help in any kind of way, but everything had been taken care of. I should have walked out and sat on a bench outside—that would have helped the awkward silence—but I waited for them to figure out what to do with me. I was told to wait in the lobby and let them decide what to do. About thirty minutes later, one of them came out and said that he was going to take me out to eat! How could I pass up hot, delicious chicken from an actual restaurant?

You must understand that while I was out there on the streets that my heart was aching for the poor and that I had set out to change the world! We talked about my trip while we ate. I told him thoughts on God's idea of changing the world. "How do you change the world?" he asked. I may have sounded harsh at the time, but with excitement in my voice, I said that it's through relationships and that if I could, I would convince the people who call themselves Christians to focus more attention on one-on-one relationships and showing people that we care and less attention on putting together large events such as concerts, church yard sales, and even the worship service. Large events are necessary, but our culture forces us to focus on the logistics of everything. It must be perfect or people are not going to come. The funny thing is that if the event is attractive enough, a lot of people will show up and everyone will be too busy to truly see the people that came. I really do love large events, but it's dangerous if our church lives revolve around them. It is very easy to get caught up in them when we equate numbers with success.

By the time we got back to the church, I still had a couple hours to kill. He said that he didn't know where I could go. Eventually he found a small room next to the lobby for me. I asked if he could get me when it was time because I didn't have a watch. When he came in to get me, he politely reminded me of what time the church opened and advised me to wait to come at that time in the future. I laughed in my head and thought, "Okay, next time I come, I'll have to leave four hours before service rather than seven."

I absolutely loved the small group meetings after the worship service! That was one of the ways that God gave me the strength to keep going. I loved being able to talk about what was going on in my life and to hear what was going on in others' lives. That's the beauty of small groups: everyone gets to talk.

One of the guys offered to take me back downtown, and I gladly accepted because it's one thing to sleep on the streets through the night, but to just roam the street in my neighborhood was not very safe because it would appear that I was looking for something. I made him drop me off a couple blocks away because I didn't know what John and Mikey would say. They knew where I went on Mondays, but they never wanted to go, which played toward my advantage because people might let out my secret. Fortunately, they weren't suspicious.

Day 17

The next morning Mikey and I slipped over to the America's Mart building where we filled out a job application earlier in the week. They didn't call Mikey's Facebook girlfriend that we knew of, but when we filled out the application, they told us to come back early today to follow up. That is literally what they said, so I had no clue what to expect. Getting a job was a job in itself. I was under the impression that we would be working within a few days, but so were fifty other people who were there as well. We had to work our way through the mob of not-so-pleasant job hunters to the door so that we could add our name to the long list of people. It was a pretty miserable sight. I literally felt like dumb sheep in a field anxiously waiting to hear any news about working. We sat in the hot warehouse with fifty other smelly people who were all fighting for the same job for four hours! Finally, the employers, called "big bosses" by the people around me, came out and stood on a platform and looked down at us. "There is no work today. Come back on Saturday with black pants and black shoes." Mikey and I were more than eager to work, so this was devastating news. We had to deal with a few more days of no work. We also found out that we needed black pants and black shoes. My tennis shoes were white and my jeans were not dark enough; plus they had gaping holes. Mikey and I had to find clothes for a job we were not even guaranteed to get.

Just before going to the spot that night, John told me he found out that he has two warrants for his arrest in St. Louis, Missouri. John was about to get a good job at a Kroger supermarket a few miles away. He almost had it until the background check came in. He was at the point of giving up—meaning, being okay with staying on the streets for the rest of his life. Hope was fading just when he thought he would be getting a job and starting his life again. After getting this news, I had no words. He explained to me that ever since he tried to live a clean life, things got worse. The only way for John to be able to get a job was to go back to jail because there was no way to make bond. Tears ran down his face when he told me just how badly he did not want to go to jail. For a homeless person to be knocked down with this bad news was hard for me to hear, but all I could do was listen.

This was the catch: the warrants were enough to keep John from getting a job in Georgia, but they were so small that the police here would not arrest and extradite him. He needed to do his time in a Missouri jail but had no way to get there, so even serving out his sentence was not simple. John claimed that his charges were for some bad checks he had written a few years before. I was tempted to call someone to bring me money so that he could serve his time and get on with his life, but I restrained myself. It's kind of humorous to think that sending someone to jail would be considered a favor, but John was in limbo with little hope for change.

I used to wonder if homeless people wanted to be put in jail (so that they'd be taken care of), but from what I saw, that was far from the truth. I never saw a homeless person purposely get put in jail, but there was also not a huge fear of going to jail for a few days either. People out here like freedom. They like not having to answer to anyone. There was plenty of food in Atlanta, and it was somewhat freeing to go wherever you wanted. So jail does not give most homeless people what they want—freedom.

I was trying to figure out how to help these people the best that I could, but not much was coming to my mind. After seeing grown men in tears over and over again, it was tearing my heart apart. Once again, I was not sure how much longer I could take it.

The air was cool and the pavement was warm. It was the best weather so far. I was sound asleep at the church along with three others. I was actually happy that night, and I thought that I was going to get a decent night's sleep. What was I thinking? That I was in the expensive hotel next door? It must have been around 2:00 or 3:00 a.m. when Jack came up. I called him "Jack" because that was what he was holding in his hand: a half-empty bottle of good ol' Jack Daniels whiskey. Jack could barely walk, but he managed to kick us so that we would pay attention to him. We all woke up, but we just rolled over. This was nothing new, and we figured that he would eventually leave. He didn't! He did manage to get our attention, however, when he said, "If I wanted y'all dead, then I could have blown your heads off with a shotgun." John was the first one to sit up, but no one said anything yet. The man was asking one of us to hit him. It was very tempting. I had never been in a fight, but I thought that it might feel very fulfilling to knock this guy to the ground. One by one, we all sat up. Josh (the nineteen-year-old), reading my mind, stood up. Jack stared at me, leaned in, and motioned for me to swing at his face. I stood up at this point, not to punch Jack but to hold Josh back. I felt like a mom, and being the mom on the streets is not an easy job. After calming Josh down, Jack finally left. He was yelling and cursing while he crossed the street. Jack was only around for about fifteen minutes, but it felt like hours.

Shortly after Jack left, a woman walked by and asked us a shocking question. "Are you guys homeless?" Mikey was the first to pipe up. "No, I have a mansion down the street; I just like to sleep out here by the church every night." He busted into laughter after his smart remark. "Y'all are crazy," said the lady. Sometimes Mikey just says what I am thinking. Jack and this lady accounted for most but not all the entertainment that night.

Mikey couldn't sleep, nor could I, but he stayed up and walked around. A few minutes later, he came to me and could hardly talk because he was laughing so hard. "Eli, you won't believe it." After tonight, it would take a lot for me not to believe something. "Did you know that this church is made from the bones of Satan worshipers?" I said that I did not know that, with a confused look on my face. He told me that an older lady told him that the church where we slept and the one across the street were made out of the bones of Satan worshipers. We were both laughing about it.

Maybe because it was in the middle of the night; I don't know. Just as we were about to lie back down, the white-haired lady yelled, "It's not something to laugh about!" which made us laugh even more. I knew that I shouldn't, but I couldn't help it. She walked off and told other people the same story. This woman, like many other homeless people, is mentally ill and has greater needs than others. After she left, I tried to sleep more, but it was quite difficult, as you can imagine.

It was freeing not be a slave to the clock. I had nowhere I had to be, which forced me to focus on the moment. I usually thought about where I was going and what I was going to do next. When I got there, I thought about what's next. In my normal life, I was never completely finished. There was always homework, piano practice, work, class, church, and so on lurking around, so to have nothing to do was a new experience for me. The question was, how do I live in the present? I now had absolutely nothing to think about doing in the near future (for the most part), so I was forced to enjoy life in the present or basically go insane. For the most part, I did not need to know the time, but I would sometimes have to ask passers-by for the time. One day a man was walking toward us, and before we could even say, "You got the time?" he answered, "No, I have none . . . wait, the time? It's 12:30." Another lady that I asked rudely said "NO!" shortly after looking at it herself. I came to expect rejection.

Day 18

Splat! Not a sound that anyone wants to hear while sitting on the sidewalk with their back against a building. I knew exactly what it was. I looked on my shoulder to find bird droppings sitting there. Fortunately I wasn't trying to stay clean. I simply shook my head and found a napkin in my bag that I had saved for such an occasion. When I stood up, I looked up to see the line of pigeons on the gutter. It appeared as though they were aiming at people. So I stood up in the line at Safehouse to avoid the firing squad.

Day 19

There is a church right next to the capital that caters to homeless peoples' needs. They have a phone to use, bathrooms, an eye clinic, and provide help with finding just about anything one might need. We waited there for about an hour and a half for a cereal bar and a cup of Gatorade.

While we waited, we met two young guys who wanted to hang with us for a while. They were both new to the streets but were used to a rough life. They met each other just a few days prior. As if John, Josh, and Jack were not enough *J* names to keep up with, both of their names were John as well. I will refer to them as "Twenty-One" and "Nineteen" (their ages). I knew it was going to be a long day because Nineteen reminded me of some of the eight-year-old kids I used to play games with at church. His attention span lasted around 2.4 seconds, and he wanted to fight people for no reason. He would yell at people and make fun of them even if he did not know them. If someone was fat, Nineteen would let him know it. I am honestly not sure how he survived his first few days on the streets. He wore a black sleeveless shirt with army pants, and his topic of choice was marijuana. His friend, Twenty-One, was a little more tolerable. He was kind of quiet, but he always wanted to be on the go.

They both tried to make money by selling cigarettes on the street. It actually works though because most people out here can't afford a whole pack, but they can afford to buy a single cigarette for a quarter. The trick is not to smoke them. They had trouble with that part, though.

After we got our cereal bar, we did the usual and we headed toward Central Library. John went to Safehouse, and Twenty-One and Nineteen came with Mikey and me. Mikey got on the computer for a couple of hours, and I started to read and write at my usual table. Nineteen and Twenty-One sat across from me and talked about doing drugs the entire time. I could not focus, so I just closed my Bible and journal to talk with them. They could not wait to get out of the library, so I told them that they could leave whenever they wanted to, but I was going to stay until Mikey was finished.

Once Mikey was done at the computer, we took off for lunch. Lunch that day was about an hour walk. That hour felt more like half of a day because of Nineteen. I thought that my life was in danger just by being around him. When we got in line to eat at the church, we were forced to sit in different spots. Mikey and I were able to sit together, though. We started making a plan to get rid of Nineteen and Twenty-One. We saw them walk out and so we decided to take our time, hoping that maybe they would leave on their own. Just when we were about to get up, our hopes were let down: Twenty-One walked through the door. We looked for back doors, but there were no other options. Twenty-One came up to ask us what we were doing. We told him the truth. "Dude we are trying to escape the other John. You're cool, but he is gonna get us killed," said Mikey. "Can I come with y'all? I have been trying to leave him ever since I met him," said Twenty-One. Mikey and I looked at each other. "Sure," I said, "but you have to help us get rid of John." He agreed, and the childish grin on his face and funny little giggle made me realize how happy he was to join us. The people who you choose to associate with can make or break life, not only out here but anywhere. The staff was directing us to the left side of the church, which Twenty-One informed us is where Nineteen was waiting. We asked the man in charge if he would let us out a different way. He didn't let us at first, but when we told him why, he chuckled a bit and let us out a different way. We were home free! I felt like a bird that was let out of a cage. I didn't have to fear for my life as much without Nineteen around. I know it's not the most righteous thing to do, but when we saw him from a couple blocks away trying to spot us, we jumped in the bushes and laughed because he hadn't seen us. By getting Nineteen out of the picture, I had a better chance of introducing Twenty-One to Christ. I didn't shove the Gospel down his throat—he got that enough out here—but I did try to show him with my actions.

While walking half the day to get food and trying to ditch Nineteen, we still needed to get clothes for work. Samaritan's Purse was the place to get them, and fortunately it was on our way back downtown. We had tried to get clothes the day before, but we found out that we needed a voucher, which we got from Safehouse. In order to get clothes from a clothing closet, we had to prove that we needed them. The nasty clothes that we had on were not proof enough. This is a good example of how difficult it can be to complete simple tasks when living on the streets. In order to even be considered for a job, we needed to have the right color clothes. In order to get the right clothes, we had to have a voucher. Finding out we needed the right color clothes, knowing that we needed a voucher, and getting the clothes would have been easier with a phone and a car. After walking so far, it was disappointing to find out that we didn't have what we needed. We brought Twenty-One along with us because he had nowhere else to go. When we found the clothing room at Samaritan's Purse, it was almost fun. I shopped for my black pants and black shoes. The pants that I got were probably worth more than any pants that I had ever bought before. They were brand-new Express pants and the pockets were still sewn together. The only problem was that they wore a size 36/32 and I wore a 30/32. Unfortunately, the store didn't have any belts. I was forced to wear my green strap belt, but why should I care: I lived on the streets, after all. I used to think that homeless people had no right to be picky. I still believe that to an extent, but I don't believe that we should just give away our leftovers. Homeless people get leftover everything—leftover food, leftover clothes, leftover shelter, and leftover time. Not always, but more often than not, I could tell that the people taking care of me were more interested in getting out of there. The people at Samaritan's Purse were good to me. They helped me pick out shoes, too. I got black and white imitation Converse All Stars, but they were anything but comfortable.

After cramming the new clothes in my bag, the three of us walked back downtown. Along the way, we rested by one of Georgia State University's entrances. While we were sitting on a bench, Mikey kept staring at the college girls piling out in front of us. Twenty-One thought that it was a little strange when I was getting on to Mikey for staring at the girls. Mikey has two big problems; weed and women. He seems to get into trouble with both. I was simply trying to help him out.

The conversation then headed to sex, and Twenty-One was full of questions. He was confused that I put forth an effort to not stare at the beautiful girls. After a while of talking to Twenty-One, he just stopped midsentence and said, "Wait, so you're still a virgin?" He had this blank look on his face as he waited for an answer. "It ain't easy, but yeah, I am," I said. He could not get it through his mind that someone my age was still a virgin. Then he said, "By choice?" I kind of laughed, "Yep." Mikey explained to Twenty-One that he thought it was cool that I was committed to my beliefs. My words had a weight to them that they would not normally have. God often uses a blameless lifestyle to speak to others in a strong way. Twenty-One sat there in a daze for a few minutes because he simply could not believe what I said. I believe that is one of the problems facing the church today: Who wants to be part of something that is so different than they are? "How blessed are those whose way is blameless, who walk in the law of the Lord" (Psalm 119:1). What is the difference between the world and Christians?

Later at Safehouse, "Grave Digger," a hot-headed man whose muscles were as big as his ego, came storming into the parking lot yelling and cursing at Crystal, a girl alleging that Grave Digger raped her. I say that in the nicest way possible, but she put it differently. I was also told that Grave Digger was involved with a large gang, which was not surprising. So far, I had avoided fights, and I wanted to keep it that way. I kept my distance as I watched Grave Digger grab a nearby crutch, break it into a two-foot piece, and slam it into the wall right above Crystal's head while yelling. The police showed up pretty quickly and put a stop to him before anyone got hurt. It was just another day in the neighborhood. Sadly, this kind of occurrence became the new norm.

When we were inside listening to the music, a man asked the crowd if anyone could play the piano. Mikey knew that I did, so he was jumping up and down like an idiot pointing both index fingers at me. The man looked at me and asked if I wanted to practice with a group from his church a few miles away. I missed playing the piano and so I said that I would love to. He told me to show up at his church around 7:00 p.m. the next Monday, so I said "Okay, I'll be there." I thought it was strange that he asked me. I mean, didn't he know that I didn't have a car? I would have to skip going to Safehouse, but I might as well experience as much as possible while I was on the streets. This would give me another chance to see how outsiders would view me.

Day 20

"Screen on the Green": I had seen it advertised all week. Centennial Olympic Park showed different movies once every two weeks for free on a huge outdoor screen. It wasn't far from Safehouse, and Mikey was planning on going because if we stayed long enough after people were gone, the nonalcoholic drinks were free. We planned on meeting back up with Twenty-One because he left us after the Samaritan's Purse, but it was a lost cause. Thousands of people were already there by the time we arrived. It was almost impossible to walk around, much less find a place to sit. With no cell phones, we weren't able to find Twenty-One anywhere. I actually never saw him again. I did, however, run into Donnie, the slow-talking Caribbean guy from the park. He was trying to sell some paintings of his. It was good to see him, but we didn't talk much because the people sitting on the ground were complaining about not being able to see. He was busy trying to get money, so we parted ways. I did get a chance to ask him about Larry, but he hadn't seen him in a few days.

The only place available for us to sit was in the trees, where I could only see half of the screen and the only thing we heard was the crowd. In order to get a free drink, we would need to stay until later, and I was not looking forward to it. I was exhausted and it was not worth a Powerade to stay up, so I went "home." I found out that someone else had already taken our spot, which forced me to look for John and see if he had any ideas. I found John behind the animal statues down the street in the not-so-good neighborhood, so we decided to camp out there for the night and take our chances without protection from the doorway and streetlights.

Day 21

With both hands wrapped around a blue Powerade, I woke up to the sunrise. The only good thing about the place behind the animal statues is that the Ambassadors take a little longer to get there. When I sat up, I saw that Mikey and Josh were there, too. I recalled Mikey getting there late last night. "Here ya go little buddy," he handed me the drink while I was sleeping. Not thinking, because I was asleep, I sat the drink to the side of me on the pavement. "You can't do that," said Mikey, "You have to hold on to it." And that's how the drink got there. I slept with my head on my backpack and my shoes and drink in hand. Anything not touching me while I slept would have been gone by morning. Mikey did tell me that someone tried to take the shoes off of his feet one time, so nothing is very secure, but I did my best. Sometimes I would forget about my water bottle and it would be gone, even if it was right next to me. It did have its conveniences though. If we had any leftovers that we didn't want (which was not often), we would just set them next to us and they would be gone in the morning; no need to walk to the trash can. Leftovers don't do well without a refrigerator, so holding on to food was almost pointless.

Day 22

Mikey and I were waiting patiently for Saturday to arrive to see if we could work. He was eager to work for money, and I was eager to wear my new outfit in public! Again, Mikey and I arrived at the warehouse a couple of hours before work because we wanted to make sure that we were the first people there, but there were already about fifteen people by the time we arrived, and no one was guaranteed to work. I went through the trouble of getting clothes, showing up early twice, and I still didn't think that I was going to find work. At around 7:45 a.m., the big bosses came out and stood over the crowd of about fifty people once again. This time they did need workers, though. "We need ten people to go with Claire." Hands started going up all over the place, even though the boss man made it clear to keep our hands down. He started looking through the crowd and pointing to different people to come and work. One person that the boss picked didn't have black pants on, so they had to leave. After the first ten people were picked, my hope began to fade. "Okay, now we need ten more people to go with Jane." Mikey said, "He better pick us or I'm gonna be ticked off." I agreed and just stared at the boss man politely. "You and you," the boss said while pointing at Mikey and me. Finally, we were able to start work! All our hard work was about to pay off. Two or three people got picked after us, and the boss said to the rest of the thirty people, "That's all we need today, come back tomorrow and maybe you can work."

I honestly do not know how they picked people, but I don't see how it can be by appearance. I was wearing a black Georgia Bulldogs hat with paint on it, and my dirty face had an untamed beard attached to it. Mikey and I started heading up the ramp, and they asked us our names and made sure we were wearing our black pants with black shoes. As goofy as I looked, I passed the test and was able to work.

They handed the ten of us gray polo shirts with the company's name on it. I just changed right there in front of everyone. I couldn't wear my hat, so I peeled it off of my nappy head and tried to shake my hair free from the mold of the hat. We also had to tuck our shirt tails in. I had to fold the pants over in the front for my belt to latch. I felt ridiculous as it was, but it only got worse. I thought that I would be setting up tables for a conference before the business people arrived. You know, out of sight from the real world. But all that I was told was that I would be taking out the trash all day. I did not know that it was for a huge fashion show with twenty-one floors of beautiful models walking around with millionaires, searching for the next line of clothes to choose for their company. Gap, Express, Limited Too, and many more clothing companies were there looking at clothes to decide what to purchase for their stores. I already felt pretty low at this point, and I didn't need anyone else to look down on me. But I felt even lower because I was surrounded by rich people.

I had to patrol the trash cans on the eleventh floor and Mikey had the thirteenth. The building was open in the middle, and I could see all the way to the top. My job was to walk around the entire building and check the trash cans. There were also two other people on the eleventh floor with me: a male and female assigned to clean the four bathrooms on that floor. My floor wasn't that busy, which made my job extremely boring. My shoes hurt, and I walked around for a few hours changing about one trash bag per hour. I would have rather been busy taking out the trash, but I didn't have much of a choice. Time went by slower and slower.

We were given a thirty-minute lunch break to eat, but there was only one problem: thirty minutes is not nearly enough time to get food from a soup kitchen. But there was hope. I managed to grab a cup of ramen noodles from the dumpster the night before at Safe-house. Mikey had a cup too, and when we met for lunch in the garage, we pulled out our cups. These are the cups of soup that already have the spices mixed in; all you have to do is pour hot water in them. That was the problem: we didn't have any water, much less hot water. There were water fountains upstairs, but the trip up would take the rest of our time. I ate about two bites of my crunchy soup, and if I didn't know better, I would have thought that I had bitten into tiny twigs with mold surrounding them. I couldn't take it. Mikey was going to town on his though. I asked him to try mine just to see if his was better than what I had. When he tried it, he spit it out. "That's nasty," he said and gave me the rest of his. It was Saturday, so we didn't get breakfast from Mrs. Kay. I was supposed to last until 6:00 p.m. with nothing but a few bites of raw ramen noodles to hold me over all day. My last meal was the night before at about 6:30, and between not having much sleep, walking for hours, and standing for hours, my body began to feel weak by 11:30 a.m.

Before I knew it, lunch was over and I was working again. I didn't think that the time could go by any slower, but when my stomach started growling, it just about stood still. I stopped at every water fountain to try to fill up with that, but it was no use. My hands were shaking, and I had a horrible headache. I had to keep walking in the circle mindlessly. I didn't know if I was going to be able to get food at Safehouse because we were pressed for time. I was far from starving to death, but I had never felt that bad from hunger before. As my feet dragged by a trash can, there it was sitting right on top of the trash: a half-eaten bowl of pasta salad. I look around to make sure that no one was looking, put the small bag into my big one, and wheeled it to the nearest bathroom. I glanced to my left and then to my right. I checked to see if anyone was in the bathroom. Then I quickly grabbed the bowl, ran into the bathroom, and locked the door. I stared at the bowl of pasta thanking God for skinny models that can't finish their bowl of food and shook my head saying, "Here it goes," as I dug in. I ate every noodle, tomato, cucumber, and olive (I don't even like olives) with my hands. I felt a little savage, but it didn't matter. Even though I didn't get full from it, the bowl of pasta gave me what I needed to make the job a little less miserable. I was actually pretty excited to see what would be in the trash the next day. This marks one of my lowest points: living on food out of trash cans.

It was 5:00 p.m. when the boss asked me to stay for another three hours. I hadn't eaten since the pasta salad around 2:00 p.m., but I didn't have much of a choice. She told me that she had been watching me and was impressed with how good I was doing and chose to let some others go early. Now I had two floors to look after: eleven and twelve. Why did I do so well? I didn't know that anyone could fail at walking around and looking in trash cans, but I was wrong. Actually, Mikey was one of the ones who left early. I just hoped that he would save me some food from Safehouse. The time moved a little quicker because I had two floors, but I once again had a headache and shaking hands due to hunger.

It was about a twenty-minute walk to Safehouse, and if I made good time, I might be able to get a sack of food. After work, I started heading over. This was by far, the longest twenty-minute walk ever. When I walked through the gate, I saw Mikey, John, and Jay sitting in the parking lot just finishing their meal. Jay was a quiet guy who wasn't exactly homeless, but he hung out with us and ate with us on occasion. Jay knew how hungry I was, so he handed me his gummy bears dessert. They were the best gummy bears ever! There was a line forming for seconds, but there was no guarantee that I would get any. Standing in that line was torture. Finally, I got a plate and scarfed it down before I made it back to where Mikey and John were sitting. I hoped that if I got picked the next day to work, I would find more food in the trash to eat.

Before we headed to the spot, we stopped in a park to shoot the breeze for a while. I am a pro at shooting the breeze. No matter what I saw out here, I still couldn't help but to stare at some of the things that went on. I found out that sometimes there is no need for a bathroom. I saw a man walking down the sidewalk, people all around, urinating in a cup as he walked. I don't think that he was in a hurry either. When he was done, he simply poured out the waste in the grass and kept walking. I was getting used to being surprised every day.

Chapter 7

Mikey Knows

Day 23

I had to be at work by 9:00 that morning, but I still had to go through the selection process before starting, so there was no guarantee that I would actually work. Fortunately, my small boss, Jane, liked me and picked me again. She also picked Mikey, which proved to me that he must not have done too poorly the day before. We went through the routine of changing into the gray shirt (we had to return them at the end of the day) and swallowing my pride as I walked into the fashion show looking and smelling worse than horrible.

I was the lucky soul that got stuck with Debra that day. The bathroom cleaners had to stay with each other no matter what (why, I do not know), and Debra walked slower than my friend Donnie talked. Any slower, and I am sure that we would be walking backward. Besides the stomach pain due to hunger, Debra seemed to make the day go by even slower than the day before. I didn't even have a cup of dry noodles, so by lunch I was really hungry. Luckily, I was assigned to the seventh floor, which had more people. And more people meant more opportunity for food, hopefully.

While working I saw a beautiful sight: a pizza box sitting next to the trash can. I was in charge of cleaning the bathrooms, but I could still pull off being a trash collector. "Lord, please let there be a piece of pizza in that box. Please, Please, Please!" I prayed. While Debra was sleeping in the lady's room (she confessed to me later), I grabbed the pizza box and opened it. I was so excited to see that someone did not like their slice of pepperoni pizza. They had only taken one bite before throwing it away. I closed the box and couldn't keep from smiling while I checked the bathroom to make sure no one was using it. When it was clear, I snagged the pizza, hid it in my hand, and ran inside and locked the door behind me. It was cold but very satisfying! I later found a Hooters box and hoped for some half-nibbled wings. I found only a couple chips with cheese that had already hardened, but they were still tasty. After lunch time, the food slacked off before I was completely full.

Debra had her good moments, but for the most part, it was difficult to work with her. She would talk about praising God but then curse out other people under her breath the next sentence. Most of the people that I worked with said they wanted to work for as many hours as they could in order to get more money, but once they started working, they would complain about doing the work. Most of them would rather sit around. Speaking of sitting around, the employers actually have a problem with people sitting around instead of working. I didn't sit very often, but my boss told me it was okay to rest every now and then. Plus my shoes were killing me. A different boss happened to come around the corner and see me while I was sitting. "Oh, are you just tired or something?" he said with a sarcastic tone. I wanted to tell him that I had no intention of being there and that I didn't like to be talked to like that, but I just said, "Yep," and started walking again. I got off at 7:30 p.m. and made it to Safehouse just in time to eat. Dinner had never tasted better!

Day 24

The next day, I did it all again, despite how exhausted I was. I was so tired from work that I didn't care about anything except food and sleep, which were both scarce. Ten hours a day with very little food and a concrete mattress to sleep on made me hate working.

Mikey found me working on fifteenth floor taking out trash. "Dude, come here," Mikey said in an excited whisper. I followed him to the big dumpster on that floor next to the industrial elevator. He pulled out three hot sausage biscuits wrapped in aluminum foil that had not been touched! This was around 9:30 a.m. We were told not to take any food from the caterers, but Mikey was determined not to go hungry that day, so he asked the man preparing the food if he had any left, and the man gave him three hot biscuits. The aroma of the biscuit filled my nostrils before I sank my teeth into the warm, flaky bread. I savored every bite of the biscuit while standing next to the large, smelly dumpster. Mikey said that the floor that he was assigned to was loaded with food. I planned to meet him up there for our lunch break. "I'll hold on to the third biscuit so we can split it for lunch," Mikey said. He later told me that he couldn't stop himself from eating the whole thing, but I knew that would happen.

When lunch time came around, I headed up to the nineteenth floor to find Mikey. He told me that his pockets were full of food. I was so happy! I didn't know what he had, but I couldn't wait to find out on the balcony. He started pulling out cookies, chips, and then I saw a chicken salad sandwich, all of which he found in the trash can. I prayed before we ate: "Thank you Lord for this food!" Even though the prayer was said as my face met the food, I have never been as sincere as I was about that meal. Before I took the first bite, I remembered Mikey telling me a few days ago that we were blessed. My heart began to break for people around the world who didn't have what I had, even on the streets. The less I had, the more I saw a huge, huge need elsewhere to the extent that I wanted to do something about it. Here I was, eating out of a trash can and being more thankful than ever because I was blessed to eat.

Homeless was not the way I felt on the fifteenth-floor balcony because I had enough food to get full, and I had a pretty sweet view of the city. I could see the park with the Olympic fountains and watch the people walking on the streets below. I was fairly comfortable until Mikey asked me a question after a long silence. This was the question that I dreaded to hear.

"Eli, why are you really out here?" Oh, no; he's on to me. How did he know? What was I going to say? "I mean, you don't smoke anything, you don't drink, you don't curse, your attitude is good, and you are always studying the Bible." I said, "Okay, okay, but you have to promise not to tell anyone." I didn't want people to think that I had money or that I was trying to mock them. He tried to guess why I was there before I could get it out. "You ain't runnin' are you?" "No! Haha! I'm not running." I paused and became serious. "Basically, I came out here because God told me to so that I would be able to trust and rely fully on him to take care of me, and to gain others' perspective. I have a car, and I am going back to my school in southern Georgia in the fall." I'll spare you all the details, but I told him everything about who I was. "Holy sh#$, you little motherf#@$er." There was a small pause, and then he spoke up again, "Dude, you are closer to God than I thought." I wasn't sure how to take that because he already knew who I was as far as my relationship to my heavenly Father, but he meant well. He followed with, "I mean, to listen to God tell you to go somewhere and actually do it! That's pretty cool." I could breathe once again! He wasn't going to try to hold me ransom or tell all our friends that I was a lying punk and beat me half to death. I wanted to tell Mikey everything for some time now, but I didn't know how he would respond. After lunch, we just went back to work on our separate floors like nothing had happened.

Mikey needed to pick up some extra hours at work, but I didn't. The bosses, along with Debra, my bathroom cleaning partner, thought that I was so generous when I offered to give Mikey my hours. It was not as generous of a deed as they thought because little did they know, I didn't need the money. When I told Mikey that I would leave in order for him to stay and get more hours, he looked at me and said, "Are you sure, man?" He still couldn't get past the truth that I didn't need money despite what I just told him. He was so used to me being just like him: you know, homeless with a need to work. I pulled him to the side and said, "I don't even need any of this, remember?" "Oh, yeah, that's right." I was glad to leave that place, although I felt sorry for Mikey because he was now stuck with Debra. Mikey did not put up with anything. I can only imagine how he got along with her.

Everything worked out great with trading hours with Mikey because that was the day that I had been asked to play the piano at a nearby church; "nearby" meaning that I could walk to it in a few hours. Since I had eaten the cookies and the chicken salad sandwich, I had enough energy to make it. To have enough energy to make a trip was something that I had never had to think about before, but food was similar to gas. Before going somewhere, I had to make sure I was full enough to make the trip back or at least fuel up for the trip back. I was banking on the people at the church feeding me somehow so that I could make the trip back downtown since this meant I would miss my meal at Safehouse.

After about two and a half hours, I made it to the church with about fifteen minutes to spare. That was my second time seeing the church. The first time was on my way to Bethany's house for grilled cheese sandwiches. I noticed a homeless man sleeping on the front porch both times. I didn't see any cars parked out front, so I walked around to the back. Once again, I felt out of place. Sweat glazed my bare arms and hairy face, and I smelled horrible, but I was starting to get used to not caring about what others thought of me. Actually, more people just ignored me altogether than gave me strange looks, which made it easier on my pride. I asked the young man unloading cymbals from his old beat-up Honda if I could help him. He politely said yes. I went on to tell him that I was there to play the piano with them that night. "Did you hear about the gig online?" he asked. "Nope, the pastor asked me if I would come and practice with y'all tonight." I told him that I knew nothing about what was happening. I purposely forgot to mention where I heard from the pastor. I honestly just wanted to play the piano a little bit.

I found out his name was Brandon, and he introduced me to the lady in charge. This was actually a paid position that I was trying out for. I hadn't known that I was trying out for anything when the pastor first told me about the gig. He was extremely vague when he told me to come by the church. I watched the band set up and the people getting ready to sing. I learned that these people were putting on a show once a month to minister to kids in the area.

Their first show was just two weeks away, and they still needed a pianist. While the singers were getting the songs together, I changed into my shorts and flip-flops in the tiny bathroom. The aroma that boiled out of my tennis shoes was deadly, but my feet felt so free that I didn't care how they smelled. I tied my shoes to my pack and waited in the sanctuary until things started up.

Brandon asked me a lot of questions, but I tried to remain as quiet as possible. I honestly didn't want to explain my situation, but then came the question: "Where ya stayin' at?" Great, now I had to tell him that I was homeless. "Right now I'm on the streets, but I don't think that it will be for long." I left it at that, and he took it from there. He knew that I had not been on the streets for long, but his whole attitude changed. At first, Brandon kept the conversation light, and I didn't drive the conversation at all. Once he found out that I was homeless, all his energy and attention was focused on me. The care that he showed me with his words was refreshing and beautiful. Band practice still hadn't started, but Brandon told me that he wanted to pray with me before I left for the night.

By the time practice was over, I was getting pretty hungry and started to consider sleeping there at the church with the other homeless person. Brandon pulled me aside and started telling me about his life. He told me of a time just a couple of years ago where he was addicted to drugs and was almost homeless himself. God began to work in his life and now he lives his life trying to serve God. Hearing his story was especially encouraging to me because I could see that God really does change people. I was already emotionally moved by this point when his story got even better. Brandon is the father of two little girls, and he was still married to the mother. He moved to Atlanta to pursue a music career, which is no easy task, but he wasn't having any luck. He was struggling to get by and was even on the verge of going hungry, but he was doing what he loved and was called to do. He pulled a crumpled five-dollar bill out of his pocket. "I try to go on a date with my wife every month, and this was saved up for that occasion, but I want to give it to you because you are in need more than I am." I wanted to cry right there because

I saw the compassion in his heart. I was reminded of when Jesus told the disciples that the lady who gave one coin had given more than those who gave a lot because she gave everything she had.

Before I left, Brandon walked me through the small church into a room where the others were eating pizza. He asked me if I had eaten anything, and I told him not since lunch (I didn't mention that lunch was from a trash can). He placed the last two hot slices on a paper plate and told me to enjoy, and boy did I ever! Hot pizza to a homeless man is like paradise. While I was eating the pizza, Brandon explained my situation to two other people the best he could. I didn't intervene. He told them that I was on the streets and that he knew that I was a good person by the way that I spoke. All three of them took me in the sanctuary and prayed for me. I actually felt completely homeless by this point, and I needed their prayers. The lady also handed me twenty dollars before I left. I had one more day of work, which meant eating out of a trash can, but after getting the money, I did not have to anymore! Brandon ended up taking me home when he found out that I was planning on walking back.

These people were so willing to help me. It was encouraging to see them want to take care of me. Many times, Christians will help the poor when they are staring them in the face but are not willing to seek out the poor. They wait for the poor to beg before doing anything. Jesus was proactive about ministry, and we should be too. It is not always easy to serve others in need; in fact, it is rarely easy. I do know that the people on the streets who really want help and really want to do better are not the ones who will ask for it. I would even say that for every homeless person that is begging, there are ten more homeless people that will not beg but need our help just as much as the beggar. We just need to find them.

When I returned to the doorway, I was pretty excited. I had twenty-five bucks in my pocket, which made me the richest person I hung out with by far. I sat down with Mikey and John before going to sleep. While we were sitting there in the doorway, Mike, the priest in training, made his way toward us. "Hey, guys," Mike said. We said "Hey" back, and he asked us if he could fill up our water bottles. Before he left to fill them up, he talked with us for a while. He found out that we were working and didn't have food, so he offered to bring us little bags with food in it for us. He walked to his apartment nearby and brought back three bags of food. There was just enough in each bag to give us one meal. He also gave us a half-empty jar of peanut butter. You can't beat peanut butter on the street! Before going home for the night, he offered to wash some of our clothes the next evening. This is the type of person who had the biggest impact on me: while he was on his way home, he stopped by to see if he could help in any way.

After the long eventful day, there was always an eventful night to follow. This night was no exception, but we all managed to sleep through it somehow. The three of us woke up the next morning with paintball splatters on the door just above our heads. Thankfully, none of the paintballs hit us, but they were inches above our heads.

Day 25

To wait in line at McDonald's and ask for something more than a small cup of water (which was usually refused) felt like a cause for celebration—something like a sports fanatic must feel when he is waiting to get inside the Super Bowl with fifty-yard-line seats. Nothing could wipe the smile off of my face. When it was my turn to order, I was so excited to say, "Four sausage biscuits, cinnamon melts, and four waters." Mikey, John, and Josh waited patiently at the table on the other side of the long line. Putting the tray down on the table, I thanked God for the meal and we all dug in. For some strange reason, the hot food tasted better than just about anything that I have ever eaten. Honestly, the food out of the trash can was probably better quality than my breakfast for the day, but there was something about being able to pay for it and share what I had with my friends that gave me such pleasure. For the past three days, I had survived on someone else's trash. I wrote the following in my journal after eating a biscuit and a couple bites of cinnamon melts: "God taught me something through those days of eating from the trash can, but now He provides in abundance." I considered the dollar menu abundant!

We had a day off from working because the fashion show was over, but our supervisors liked Mikey and me so much that they offered us a different job with their janitorial services. I decided to take it even if it was just to get the experience of working a night shift while living on the streets. Working a night shift with nowhere to sleep in the day is not the best idea, but I guess I wasn't out there to experience good ideas.

On my day off, a youth group from out of town came to Safehouse for the week. After the service that Tuesday night, the youth spread throughout the parking lot of homeless people to sit with them and get to know them. I knew what they were getting into, but they had no clue. I didn't make it any easier for them either. I wanted to see what they were made of and I wanted this to be a growing experience for them, as it was intended. A teenager sat down next to me and a few other homeless people and started talking. The shaking in his voice told me how nervous he was, but I didn't give him much slack. I told him my name, and he asked me if I knew Jesus. "Yeah . . . yeah, I do," I replied. I didn't tell him anything else. My answers were short and sweet, just like those of many other homeless peoples. Maybe that was mean of me, but I was honestly trying to help him learn how to approach people; plus, I really was not in the mood for someone to talk to me about my spiritual condition on a deep level. I can see it now—I get all excited about what God is doing and then tell the teen how much I am blessed by God and that is why I am here. Maybe that would have been better. I don't know. Nonetheless, I was short with him.

After I responded to the teen's question about whether I know Jesus, he looked a little shocked and didn't really know what else to say. His initiative was great and he had guts, that's for sure, but it felt like the only reason he fed me and sat down to talk was to ask if I was a Christian, which is what he was trained to do. It's not bad, but it's also not a very warming approach.

The teenager asked if he could pray for me. "Sure," I said and bowed my head while he prayed for me. I can't remember his prayer, but the conversation didn't last long after. I am happy to say that later in the week, a lot of the youth got to know some of us and showed us the care and love that people need.

Day 26

Can you imagine planning half of your day, or at least a few hours of your day, to go eat somewhere and when you get there, the restaurant is closed with nowhere else to eat? That's what happened to about 230 homeless people on the Wednesday night before Mikey and I left for our first night shift. Usually, we would see a few vans full of food pull up about thirty minutes before the service started. "You think we are gonna be able to eat tonight?" "It don't look like it." I listened to other peoples' conversations about how we were not going to eat that night because the church didn't show up to feed us. The visiting youth group was still there while this was going on. They didn't have the means to feed 230 hungry homeless people either, so they were in a difficult position. A few people left, but most stayed because they had no other choice if they didn't want to go to bed hungry. I stayed even though I had twelve dollars left from the people at the church. Finally, someone stepped out of the building and said that the church would not be there to provide food that night.

I thought that there would be a small riot, but a look of extreme disappointment and sadness washed over everyone, except for a hot-headed lady who could not stop screaming at the man bearing the bad news. "How can you tell us you are sorry when you are going to eat a meal tonight and I ain't? Have you ever gone to bed hungry?" She went on for a few minutes even though others tried to calm her. Finally, the cursing stopped, and she was on her way like the rest of us. The hopeless faces that the people wore that night was heart breaking. Their expressions spoke loud and clear: "What am I going to do now? Not another miserable night!" Most of them would have to go hungry until the next day. The guy next to me in line explained how he skipped out on sleeping in a shelter and a small cup of soup to come to Safehouse to try to get a more satisfying meal. He didn't even know where to go at this point. I still can't get his face of sadness out of my mind. I did see his face light up a bit when I discreetly handed him two bucks that I had.

I found Mikey and John and told them that we were going to eat at McDonald's. My last ten dollars held all three of us over for the rest of the day. We also needed the energy to work the first night shift. After McDonald's, Mikey split up from John and me while we shopped for peanut butter and bread. The ten-dollar bill was gone, but I had what I needed to sustain me for a while. I had a couple of hours to blow before work, so what better to do than sit and talk about life. John and I decided that we were going to try to get him to St. Louis so he could serve his time and be a free man in order to get a job. I thought someone would surely help him out.

On the way to work, Mikey was acting differently than usual. I asked him what he had been smoking. "Nothing, man. You ready for work?" I wasn't buying it, though. I just hoped that our boss didn't notice anything out of the ordinary.

We made it to work early as usual, but this time we didn't have to be handpicked. We started work at 10:00 p.m. It was already dark outside, and there weren't a lot of people walking around. The crew was much smaller, and we moved to a slightly bigger building. Once again, I didn't know what I would be doing, but I knew it was work, and Mikey needed this job desperately.

Without much food or sleep, even the first hour of work was miserable. The day and night shifts have different bosses. I had two of them. One of them was a Hispanic guy who was in love with University of Georgia's football team. I imagine he spent around five hours on an elevator every day. He never really looked at me in the eye because he was so busy running around. The other boss spent time helping me get my vacuum cleaner that was the size of a small Volkswagen to work. He told me to go downstairs to get a different one, a task that was more difficult than it sounds. This was not a two-bedroom house that was vacant and dark—it was a thirty-five-story building with about ten people in it. I went to the basement where he told me to go and started humming to break the silence. I thought that sleeping on the streets was creepy, until now. Did he say left, left, right or left, right, left? After walking around the dark basement of a skyscraper for what felt like thirty minutes, I found the maintenance room, which was just as creepy as the pitch-black hallway. I grabbed the monster vacuum and headed back up the elevator. Once I reached my floor, I had to learn on my own how to use the machine because my boss was gone.

I was told to vacuum my floor and then move on to another floor when I was finished. My goal was to vacuum three floors that night. I would have loved to have an iPod that night. I don't think I had eaten enough for dinner, because halfway into the vacuuming my first floor, I began to get a headache and broke into a cold sweat. The vacuum cleaner was supposed to be self-propelled, but it felt like I was trying to push one thousand pounds of dead weight. When it was time for lunch, I found Mikey to see how things were going. I had already eaten my peanut butter sandwich, but I told him that I wasn't sure if I could finish the night. I fell asleep instantly during my first fifteen-minute break. He pushed me to keep going, so that's what I did despite nearly passing out.

The lights that were turned on were few and far between. It was enough to see what I was doing, but that was about it. They were also on a timer. I would be vacuuming and then all of a sudden the lights cut off. The red lights from the exit signs lit the way enough for me to get to the switch. I started off to the light switch walking calmly and then it hit me: there was something behind me. No, it can't be. It's all in my head. My calm walk turned into a power walk and then a jog as I could almost feel something grabbing my heels. Finally, I reached the switch and turned the light on. I'm not usually scared of the dark, but I'm also not usually alone in a skyscraper either. I even accidentally scared one of my bosses when I came around the corner.

I asked the boss if I could leave because I didn't feel well. He politely asked if I could finish the floor first, so I did and then took off for home. I pictured the doorway of the church and could not wait to curl up on what I called bed and go to sleep for a couple hours.

It was between 3:00 and 4:00 a.m. when I walked home. Up until this point, I had not roamed the streets at this hour with good reason. I saw only four people on Peachtree Street, which was a strange sight. The first two guys were walking down the street, and they asked me for money. The third guy I saw was digging in the trash can for food and asked me if I had any.

The last guy I ran into was Aaron. Aaron carried with him a large plastic bag that hung over his shoulder. As I passed by him, he asked if I needed anything. Usually only drug dealers ask this question. I shook my head, thinking of bed, and tried to keep walking, but he continued, "I've got cell phones, MP3 players, clothes, and more." I could no longer keep walking. I wanted to tell him off because I almost felt mocked by him. I turned to him, "Dude, I don't have anything, much less money!" He told me that he was also homeless, which was not hard to believe, and that he sold things for real cheap to homeless people. Why he did it at 3:00 a.m. is beyond me. He saw my worn shirt and started pulling out some clothes from his bag. "I'll sell this one for two dollars." I wanted to say, "What part of 'I don't have any money' do you not understand?" But I politely said, "Man, I really do not have any money."

I didn't feel that Aaron was a bad person, and quite frankly, I was intrigued by him. He too was interested in my life. My bed was in sight, just staring at me from a block away, but for some reason, I couldn't stop talking with Aaron. He seemed genuinely concerned for me. I know that if the majority of the people that fed me at the churches and in soup kitchens showed me and my friends as much care as Aaron did, there would no doubt be a change in their ministry. Aaron talked to me as if I had a life and as if I had feelings. He learned my name and listened to me talk. He looked at me and paused for a second, "Here man, just take this shirt. I want you to have it." I simply said, "I don't need it, but thank you." He insisted on giving me this yellow Billabong T-shirt. Usually when people on the streets act like they want to give you something, it's because there are strings attached, but Aaron knew by now that I didn't have anything to give in return. I ended up taking the shirt to replace my old one. He knew how it was to be in need, and he wanted to help out as much as he could. This was the first and last time that I saw Aaron. It was interesting how the people who have less are often more willing to give what they have than people who have more. I recalled a similar encounter while I had been living in the park and hanging out with Larry a few weeks earlier. Larry asked for things when he needed them. He asked for food, for work, for money, and for just about anything. We were sitting there in Piedmont Park when two well-dressed guys walked by. "Hey, bro, if you have an extra shirt and are coming back by here any time soon, you think you could spare one?" I wouldn't have asked for anything so boldly, but I was curious to hear what their answer would be. "We don't have any more," they said, as they walked away. I laughed a bit because I knew that they definitely did have another shirt. Why did they have to lie like that? What hit harder was thinking that I would have probably said something similar if I were in their shoes. I probably would have said the first thing that came to mind to get the beggars to quit begging.

After talking with Aaron, I finally made it to my stiff bed and crashed hard! Normally, when I get home late from a trip, I love for my face to smash into the soft pillow that nearly wraps all the way around my head. I sometimes fall asleep with my clothes on when that happens. Of course, while I was on the streets, I fell asleep with my clothes on every night, but instead of a pillow, I had my shoes, and instead of a mattress covered with blankets, I had concrete. I can honestly say that what I felt that night was no less satisfying than had I been in my own real bed. I was thankful for the doorway that John had reserved for me.

The two and a half hours of sleep that I got were hardly enough to sustain me for the day. Mikey showed up about thirty minutes before we usually woke up, just in time to get a few minutes of sleep. We normally woke up and started moving before the Ambassadors could bother us, but we overslept that day. The Ambassadors woke us up with their car horns once again. Mikey had an attitude with John, "It's your fault we overslept." John was a peace-keeper for the most part, so he just took the blame and started walking. We made it to Georgia State University's library by 7:00 a.m. I knew that I would probably get kicked out if I fell asleep, but I didn't care at that point. I found a couple of students who were already sleeping, so I decided to join in. I woke myself up three or four times snoring loudly. I could not sleep because I was paranoid that someone would find out that I wasn't just a smelly student who forgot to shower for two weeks and kick me out, so I decided to take my chances at Hurt Park. Hurt Park is right outside of the university and is full of homeless people. I could eat a lot of food on Saturdays because churches would provide meals there all day long. I knew that there were lots of homeless people there, and that was a comforting feeling. I left Mikey and John not just to find a place to sleep but to give myself a break from their childish attitudes.

Day 27

The policeman appeared to be much larger from my perspective at this point. Standing just a few inches from my head, I saw his shiny shoes and then looked up to find out that he was not very happy with my sleeping there. I must have been sleeping harder than I thought because I heard his voice fading in and out for a minute before I had enough sense to care about moving. "You can't sleep here, you have to sit up." I sat up and just stared at him for what seemed like a minute straight. I was still trying to wake up, and I simply didn't know what to say. All I wanted at that moment was to sleep, and this man was taking that from me. I had nothing to say. He eventually walked away, but he kept looking at me while he patrolled the area to make sure I did not fall asleep again.

"Ya wanna know a trick?" said a homeless lady who appeared to have been on the streets for some time but hadn't let it get the best of her. Some people just give up and try to simply survive. Others embrace their life as it is and try to make it the best they can. These people usually carry blankets and toothbrushes with them to be as comfortable as possible. That was this lady, who, although her clothes were dirty, would tuck in her shirt. I didn't really care to hear anyone's advice, but she told me I could get away with sleeping if I could lean against a tree or a wall in the park. So I found a tree and tried to get comfortable.

The kind lady asked if I wanted to go to Our Lady of Lourdes, a church that was serving hot dogs. I knew that I should go eat even though I would rather sleep at that moment. I joined her and a younger fellow that she just met earlier that day. Most of the conversation was about the fight that happened the day before. According to the lady and other people that were there, a drunk man showed up at the park looking to start trouble. Everyone knew he was another homeless man, so most people just tried to avoid him and lead him away. But one man had enough. This man found a two-by-four piece of wood and knocked the drunk guy's legs out from under him. At this point, the drunk man was begging the other guy to stop, but he didn't. Helpless on the ground, the man barring the two-by-four pounded the blunt object into his head. Blood was everywhere. The ambulance came and took him away, but from what I was told, the man died on the way to the hospital. I'm not sure if the story was true since I wasn't there, but sadly, I wouldn't be surprised if it was.

After eating at Our Lady of Lourdes and meeting other homeless people, I decided that I had had enough of the negative attitudes. I was sick of their pessimistic attitudes, and I honestly did not care to hear them. This was on Thursday, so I was eager to walk to Bethany's for grilled cheese night. This would give me a chance to unload on someone who was like-minded. I started about two hours earlier than I needed to because I would rather wait somewhere other than downtown so that I wouldn't run into other homeless people.

On the way to Bethany's, I thought about going into a restaurant to see if they would give me a pen because my last one broke the day before while I was writing in midsentence. Just as I was looking for a place to ask someone, I looked down on the sidewalk and there sat this beat-up pen. I picked it up thinking that there was no way this pen was going to work, but it turned out to be my best pen yet. It's funny how small things like that made my day so much brighter.

Along the way, I scoped out places to lay my head, because the little bit of sleep in the library and Hurt Park did not put a dent in what my body needed. I finally found a spot under some small trees off a sidewalk that was right next to I-20. I tried to lay a sweater that John gave me out on the grass, but it only slightly delayed the ants from crawling on me. I did manage to rest a little though.

As the clouds started rolling in, I searched for a place to keep my bag dry. I planned on putting the bag under the bridge while I stayed in the rain. "Please, let it rain," was my prayer. I thought to myself how refreshing it would be to get soaked, and fun too. I wish that I could say that the bottom fell out and that I had a blast getting my shower from the heavens, but reality reminded me that the sweat on my body would be the only moisture my skin would see.

John told me about the time he was sleeping in the doorway of the church when a tornado swept through downtown Atlanta a few months prior. This happened during the winter, so John had a blanket with him and hid under it, pulling it as tight as he could while broken glass and debris were making their way under the blanket. He also said that homeless people died because that storm, but I explained to him that there were no fatalities reported in the news. His response informed me that the public does not care when homeless people die and assured me that some did during the tornado. I didn't believe him at the time, but seeing the things that go on the streets made me believe that things that happen here fly under the public's radar. Also, now that I know where a lot of homeless people sleep, I don't see how it is possible that no one died the night of the tornado. Remembering that story made me thankful it wasn't storming.

The power of prayer blows my mind. James 5:16 says that the prayer of a righteous man can accomplish much. I needed to heal my heart. I wanted to care for the people that I now lived with, but I just didn't. And it was something that I couldn't make myself do. Praise God that He cares enough about us to change our hearts because He knows that we can't do it. "Lord, I don't care too much for the people that You have placed in my life. Please change that in me because I do not have the power to change me." This was the quickest answer to my prayer that I had seen. Before I was finished praying, I was in tears because I was burdened for my homeless friends so much. To this day, there is only one explanation to my changed heart: it's all God! I asked God what I could do to help my friends that I cared so much about. I felt small and helpless. His answer is what placed me on top of the world: "You are doing it." Knowing that I was in the center of God's will was the best feeling that I had ever known. I found out just how much I need God to do anything. In 1 Corinthians 12:3, it says that we cannot even call upon the name of the Lord without the Holy Spirit.

I wanted so badly to help my friends, but I knew that I was not exactly in the position to take care of them. Actually, even if I were back at home or school, I couldn't have taken care of them very well because I didn't have much money. What I could do was be there for them when they wanted to talk. I could stay up with them at night, walk with them all day, and try to understand them in ways that were impossible to do otherwise. I could also give my perspective to the church when I returned to encourage other Christians to better understand how to help others. I had zeal in me to do so much. How do Christians usually pray? I often pray for God to send someone to take care of the needs of others. "Lord, bless them; take away their hurt, hunger, or whatever the need is." How dare I pray in such a way that my only responsibility to serve others is to pray for them? "If a brother or sister is without clothing and in need of daily food, and one of you says to them, 'Go in peace, be warmed and be filled,' and yet you do not give them what is necessary for their body, what use is that? Even so faith, if it has no works, is dead, being by itself" (James 2:15–16). The author of *Compassion* puts it in words that are clearer than my own: "Prayer without action grows into powerless pietism, and action without prayer degenerates into questionable manipulation."*

After the small dark cloud passed and my nap was over, I thought I should head out to meet Bethany. I knew that she had a roommate that worked at a nearby coffee shop, so that was my destination. I tried to call Bethany the day before to make sure that she was still planning on serving, but the places that I asked would not allow me to call long distance. When I arrived at the coffee shop,

---

* Donald P. McNeill, Douglas A. Morrison, Henri J. M. Nouwen, and Joel Filártiga, *Compassion: A Reflection on the Christian Life* (New York: Doubleday, 1982), 114.

I found out that my half-day journey was in vain. Bethany's roommate informed me that she was out of town for the week. By this point, I was used to losing hours out of the day, so I wasn't too disappointed. I did take advantage of the air conditioner at the coffee shop, though. I didn't stay for too long because I had to leave about three hours before I needed to be at Safehouse for dinner. If you are keeping up, that would be six hours of walking between lunch and dinner. But hey, at least I was able to eat!

The parking lot of Safehouse was full of homeless people when I made it back downtown. There were more than usual. All the chairs were set up in the parking lot outside and there were many people serving us while music was being played. Donuts and sweet tea were being given to us as we waited for the main meal. I could feel the love from these people. They cared about *us*, not just about our bodies by simply feeding us and sending us on our way and not just about our eternal soul by giving us a hellfire-and-brimstone message before sending us away; they wanted to know about our lives. Some of them stopped and talked to us for a while, wondering what we did that day and what our plans were for the future. John, Mikey, and I were sitting in the front row toward the far left; I think it was closest to where they fill the tea pitchers. There was a young lady talking to us a good bit. I was short with my answers, but Mikey was telling her everything about his story. She was ministering to him in a way that he needed. Like I said before, the people on the streets of Atlanta know the Bible. They needed people to care about their body, mind, and soul. I believe that if you let one of these three slip away, you will be significantly less successful in ministry. Honestly, body and soul are easier to take care of because they can be easily checked off when done: "Okay, I fed them and I told them how to get to heaven." The mental care that people need is difficult because it takes a little more time, patience, and critical thinking. It is often harder to listen than it is to talk. Anyway, this young lady was doing a great job of listening. She was actually getting somewhere with Mikey, and it brought joy to my heart to see that. What happened next took the joy that I had and turned it into extreme frustration.

The speaker for the evening took the stage and called out to the girl talking with us. "Okay young lady, go sit down over there now. This is the important part of the service. It is my time to preach God's Word," said the pastor. His demeanor was unpleasant and demanding. You would have thought he was firing an employee who had stolen from him. This lady was sharing the love of Christ much more effectively than the pastor did. I couldn't wait. What he was about to say needed to be extremely powerful and moving to make up for cutting our time short. I didn't think that it could get much worse, but sadly, it did.

Walking a mile in someone else's shoes is what I try to think about while talking to others. It helps me understand and also increases my patience with others. I guess no one ever taught the pastor this saying. "Your life right now is heaven compared to hell," he preached. Even though this was true, what was he thinking that would accomplish? Earlier on in this journey, I wrote in my journal that this was hell. Of course I knew that I still had it good compared to many, but that's not what I wanted to think about while I was there. Okay, so here I was about to jump out of my seat, take the microphone, and start preaching to a few hundred homeless people like they were humans, but I refrained and only became more disappointed with his sermon. If you want to push someone away and shut them down, start by telling him his situation isn't that bad.

A small word of advice—when talking to others who are in difficult times, do not mention how bad you've had it in the past, especially when it does not compare to their situation. Furthermore, do not tell a homeless person that you're suffering because your house isn't big enough. I guess no one taught him this either. I understood his intentions, but to hear him talk to homeless people about his small home and a beat-up Chevrolet that he used to own was almost physically painful. I didn't understand what most of the people out on the streets go through, but I did know what it felt like to be hungry with no money and not even know when you were going to eat next. I did know what it felt like to be extremely exhausted with nowhere to lay your head and nowhere to sleep without being thrown in jail. I did know what it felt like to be hot and dirty with nowhere to wash up and cool off. I did know what it felt like to be lonely with no one to talk to or to look forward to talking to someone who cares even a little. I did know what all these things felt like all at once. And the worst part of it was that I always thought the next day wasn't going to be any better, and I was right! Do you think that I wanted someone to tell me that I was living in heaven? Do you think that I wanted to hear that other people suffer because of their small homes and old vehicles with family close to them? I can't remember another word that man said. I shut down after he tried to compare his bad times of living in a tiny home and driving an old truck with our situations, and I imagine I wasn't the only one. That ministry would have been far more effective if all the members simply walked around talking with the homeless one-on-one.

Later that night, John and I were sitting in the doorway of the church when I saw a familiar vehicle go by. I was used to people staring at me from inside their car, so I didn't think much of it until I caught a glimpse of the passengers; it looked like my brother and his wife. I told John that I would be right back and went to check it out. I didn't tell him anything else, though. I walked around the block to see if they would circle around. While I was waiting there on the street, they pulled up next to me. It was them! They found me while they were on their way in town. They pulled the car on the side of the road and got out to see me for a minute. That's when I realized how many homeless people were really around. At least one homeless person walked by every minute for the time we stayed there. The vehicle with clean people around it attracted them like fish in a pond are attracted to bread crumbs. They gave me some pizza, but I ended up giving the pizza to a guy who was begging for money because I wanted to visit them in peace, which was impossible. I was glad to see that Jesse and Jennifer, my brother and sister-in-law, were there to see where I lived. They insisted on giving me a few bucks even though I refused it. I ended up taking it, but I knew it would not last through the next day because I was not afraid to spend it in order to bless others. I was afraid that Josh would ask a lot of questions when I saw him walking up to the car along with his girlfriend and another guy. Fortunately they were all stoned, so they just walked by after admiring the car. That was a close call.

Day 28

I knew that my mom was going to be in town on Friday, and I was hoping I'd get a chance to see her. She was going to the Philips Arena, which was in my neighborhood. While I was looking for her, I ran into Larry close to where I was supposed to meet my mom. I had not seen him in a while, and he was full of questions. I did tell him that I was meeting my mom, but that was about it. He kept on making comments about her giving me money, so I'm pretty sure that he was just waiting around to get a meal off of me. I didn't know what time my mom's bus would arrive, so I started waiting at about 2:30 and talked to Larry for about an hour. I knew that he had to be at a shelter at least by 4:30, so I waited patiently for my mom hoping that she would show up after he left, which she did. Another close call.

Normally I would have felt uncomfortable waiting for my mom outside the doors of an arena that hosting a women's conference, but I was getting used to being uncomfortable. I was surrounded by women, and finally I saw my mom walking toward me. It was probably better for her to see me than it was for me to see her. I knew that I was okay, and I knew that she was okay, but she didn't have the convenience of knowing I was okay. My mom knew that I would not take money from her even though she probably wanted me to, but a few of the ladies that rode the bus with her handed me a few bucks. I wondered if they would have done that if they knew what I was going to use it for.

After waiting in line with my mom and talking with her for a few minutes, I made a trip to the grocery store. I'm not a fan of taking trips to the grocery store in a car, much less walking to one. While I was on the way to the store, I saw a security guard across the street from where I slept at night. He found a couple of bags that belonged to some homeless people that stayed there in the doorway of that church. I waited around to see what he was going to do with them. Would he hide them in the bush for them to find later or would he turn them in to the church? I don't know why it surprised me when he shoved all of them in the nearest trash can. Barely five minutes later, I saw someone else digging everything out.

Friday, June 27 was Mikey's birthday, and I had money to throw him a party! How exciting! That was why I made the trip to the grocery store. I arrived at Publix and started looking for a cake, but even the small ones were out of my price range. I had enough to get some cookies with icing, small birthday plates, and a candle with a two-liter bottle of soda. The trip home was long because I had to carry the groceries a couple of miles.

When I made it to the church, John was already there and Mikey was off with a girl, according to John. John didn't seem to think that Mikey would be back before the morning. I was hoping that he would be, though. I went to the liquor store across the street to get some cups for the drinks. I also purchased some cigarettes for John with the few dollars that I had left. I don't plan on justifying spending money that was given to me by sweet ladies on cigarettes for my friend, but at the time, I felt that it was okay and even the right thing to do. Was it? I don't know, but I do know that this act showed John I cared about him, and I wanted to show him that in as many ways possible. Besides, I was tired of constantly looking down in ash trays and on the sidewalk for used cigarettes that were not fully smoked. I couldn't help but to look for them because he looked for them constantly. Okay, so I guess I did try to justify it a bit. Oops.

When I returned to the doorway, I threw the pack of Newport cigarettes in John's lap. You would have thought I handed him a bar of gold. His face lit up with excitement, and he would not stop thanking me.

Mikey finally showed up before we went to sleep. I took out the candle and placed it into the cookie and icing. When I lit the candle, John and the drunken neighbors that sleep in the doorway next to us sang "Happy Birthday" to Mikey. He was so surprised and repeatedly said that this was the best birthday he had ever had. Every time I heard things like that, I realized how much longer the list was getting of things that I had taken for granted. Mikey didn't eat a single cookie because the neighbor gave him a forty-ounce beer when he found out it was his birthday. Even though he loved what we did for him, he preferred the beer over the cookies.

Day 29

Saturdays were like a vacation in downtown Atlanta for homeless people. It was like an all-day buffet at Hurt Park, which was like heaven for all of us. The police even let us take naps there because Georgia State wasn't in session. It was like a huge picnic, and the best part was that we didn't have to pack any food. We started off the day at 7:30 that morning when we, along with about two hundred others, lined up for breakfast. That's when I heard the first Gospel message of the day. After eating, the church that served gave us huge trash bags with clothes in them. Another homeless guy I didn't know insisted on giving me a red polo shirt. He said it looked like it would fit me. I figured it would also add extra padding to my current "pillow" (a.k.a. my shoes), so I took it.

It was glorious to lie down and take a nap without worrying about being put in jail or at least being rudely awakened. Between naps, I would use bread crumbs to lure the pigeons in. Hundreds of pigeons would come near. John was laying down sleeping, so I thought that it would be funny to make the pigeons land on him. I wasn't sure if they would, but the closer I threw them toward John, the more pigeons came. I threw the crumbs about five feet away and then inched them in little by little until I was throwing them on John's back. I guess John wasn't completely asleep because right when one went in for the bread, he swung his arm around, spooking the whole mob of pigeons causing a gust of wind that almost blew my hat off. Mikey and a couple others sitting on the grass started laughing. That was the entertainment of a peaceful homeless man's day.

Of course when you put two hundred homeless people in one spot all day in the heat, there was bound to be some trouble. No one was killed that day, but there were a few fights that broke out. Having lived on the streets for a few weeks, I had grown immune to a lot of violence, drug use, and pointless arguments, so most of the time, I chose not to get involved in the drama surrounding me.

After about 10:00 a.m., churches from all over the city came to feed us at the park. I could actually choose what kind of food I wanted to eat. Did I want sandwiches or donuts? There would be two or three churches at the edge of the park at one time. It wasn't much different from going to the mall with a group of friends and choosing different restaurants in the foot court. After a while, I stopped getting food because I was so stuffed. Mikey and I went to Underground to buy a deck of cards at the dollar store with some change that we had. Back at the park, we played Hearts and ate all day long. Homeless heaven only lasted so long, though. It wasn't long until I was back in the real world of walking far for meals with no sleep, but I knew that I had a paycheck coming from my job, which gave me something to look forward to. Our plan for what we were going to do with the money was priceless.

Chapter 8

Payday

Day 30

It was time to go to church! I tried to convince John and Mikey to tag along with me, but I only managed to convince Mikey. We made our way toward the capitol building on Central Avenue. We walked through the doors of a Presbyterian church, feeling out of place, as usual. People would look at us and then look away. We sat down toward the back and to the right. We had the pew all to ourselves. The music was beautiful. After a while with no MP3 player or radio, it was nice to hear music of just about any kind any chance I got.

The minister started by telling us about everything the church does to provide help to those in need. I was eager to hear what she had to say. By this point, my stomach needed a little hospitality. I was hoping that one of the things that this church did was feed visitors. I was also curious to see how the people would treat us after that sermon. In the back of my mind, I was hoping for another warm meal like the church across the street from the spot had provided.

I took my time leaving the church to satisfy my curiosity. I was also hoping to satisfy my hunger, but so far, no one invited us to lunch. Mikey knew that I was hungry, and he was too. "Eli, did you go to church to find food? That's not why you should go to church." When Mikey told me this, I didn't think that he got my point that I was also there to see how the church responded to us. He knew why I was on the streets, but he made me realize how selfish I had become. Mikey, a homeless guy who likes alcohol and drugs more than food, was teaching me about my motives for going to church. Go figure. We slowly walked out of the church, but no one spoke to us. Most of the people I tried to make eye contact with quickly turned and walked away.

I was planning on going to church with Bethany that night, but I had nothing to do in the meantime. Mikey and I wandered around Five Points, a section of downtown Atlanta, looking for food and something to pass the time. We were obviously still hungry, so we made our way to the Gateway resource center where they were handing out cereal bars. We were also hoping to take a much needed shower while we were there, which didn't end up happening. Food was a necessity but a shower was not. With our cereal bars in hand, we walked under some of the big bridges nearby and my eyes found a world that I didn't know existed.

We followed a well-worn trail through the tall grass and small trees. There was trash along the trail, and we eventually came to what some people called home. To my left was an old, rotten hammock that was still being used. Next to the hammock were a tent and another trail. A camp fire with burning trash that was in the middle of a few other tents surrounded by tall grass replaced the scent of the somewhat fresh outdoor air with smoke. There were only a couple of people there at the time. Other trails led to the other permanent campsites that made up an inner-city, third-world subdivision right under the bridges where two main interstates intersect.

It seemed like every nook and cranny of downtown had homeless people living there, and I was amazed every time I would find a new place that people called home. I had heard about an abandoned building downtown that homeless people lived in, which sparked my interest, but I didn't know the exact location. After eating our cereal bars, we made our way to Clark Library. Clark Library was the least populated public library that allowed us to use the Internet without a wait. The only problem was its location: about a two-hour walk. On our way to the library, Mikey pointed out the abandoned building. This was a place that Mikey and John never went into, and with good reason. Some of the stories that I heard on the streets were far from true, but I believe a lot of what I heard about this place. The building is located near the Philips Arena parking lot. The seven-story building was almost pitch black on the first few floors because the windows were boarded up. There was only one way into the building. On the back side was a doorway with a hole in the board that people could step through. I walked up to the entrance, but Mikey wouldn't take me inside, and I didn't think it would be wise for me to go in alone. According to Mikey, the first room is knee high in trash, needles, and people lying around. It is a dangerous place for anyone to enter. The signs on the front of the building read: "No trespassing, violators will be prosecuted." Mikey just looked at me when we passed the sign and said, "Yeah right." The abandoned building and the campsites were good examples of poverty in the middle of wealth: two extreme class brackets on top of each other. Most of the poverty is unseen.

After spending some time in Clark Library, we made our way to church. I didn't think that Mikey would want to go to church that night, let alone walk three and a half hours to get there. I would often ask myself if I was even doing any good with Mikey. Were Mikey, John, or anyone else going to change because of anything I was doing? The answer was (and still is) very clear: no! If I tried to change their lives, I would be worn out and displeased with their progress. If I allowed God to change them while I stepped out of the way, then I might actually see some change. The reason I was there at all was because God was teaching me how to step aside. That night after church, Mikey actually caught himself cursing, which was a pretty significant improvement.

When we made it back to the spot, it was already night, and we were hoping no one had taken it. Fortunately John was there, along with his attitude and none other than Jimmy. Jimmy was Josh's girlfriend's other boyfriend, if that makes any sense. The day before, Jimmy and Luna (the girlfriend) were planning on getting married, but that night, he explained to us that it was over between the two of them. We heard the same story on alternating days from Josh.

Instead of staying at home watching soap operas, I was able to live in one! Joy. The girlfriend changed guys literally far more often than I changed my underpants.

John got on our case for not being there in time to reserve the spot. He was irritated with Jimmy and blamed us for not getting there in time. "Maybe you should have come to church with us," I said. That was the wrong thing to say. He went on to tell me about the four services that he went to. I simply started to ignore him and Jimmy and talked to Mikey. The doorway would only sleep three people anyway, and it didn't look like Jimmy was leaving, so I just made my way to the side of the church to go to sleep. Before I lay down, Mikey and I made plans for what we were going to spend our paychecks on.

Being practical is definitely not a bad thing, but it's possible to be too practical when it comes to ministry. Is it more practical to feed twenty hungry people hot dogs and chips with fifty dollars or feed two hungry people a steak dinner with that money? The twenty people will be grateful, but most likely their gratefulness will dissipate into nothing because of the perceived value of their meals. The two people who received the steak dinner will most likely be very grateful and never forget the occasion. Their gratefulness is more likely to affect more people through a "pay-it-forward" attitude than the gratefulness of the twenty people who got hot dogs. Which is more practical? Spiritual food is no different. We must not try to be too practical all the time. There is room for both—feeding as many as possible and feeding few with more quality. Ask Jesus. Most of His ministry was focused on twelve men, while less of His time was spent teaching the multitude.

Money to the average homeless man is more of a temptation than help. I say that because I did not meet a single person on the streets that did not use drugs or drink alcohol. Most of the ones I met would rather have those two things than food. I'm sure there are homeless people that do not drink and smoke, but I never met them. In 2005, a documentary was made about a homeless man by the name of Ted called *Reversal of Fortune*. He was given $100,000 and free financial advisers. Ted did not use the financial advisers and within six months, he was broke again and living on the streets with more debt than before. When reading this, it did not surprise me at all. My friends would probably not do much better.

I guess what I am trying to say is that I didn't want to put the money I made in a bank account for Mikey and John, even though it crossed my mind. My check was only $180, but that was enough to cause more harm than good in their hands. Mikey and I decided that it would be worthwhile to have an amazing week of luxury with our whopping $380 combined. Here is a list of some of the activities we had planned for the three of us:

1. Visit the Six Flags theme park.
2. Go to an Atlanta Braves baseball game.
3. Go to a couple movies and the theater.
4. Eat dinner at Sun Dial (a restaurant with dinner plates averaging thirty dollars, located on the top three floors of the seventy-three-story Weston Hotel, that rotates and gives guests a panoramic view of Atlanta).

I was looking forward to that last one just to see the looks we would get. I figured that by the time we got through the list and a couple of McDonald's runs, we would be broke again, but none of us would ever forget the vacation, and that would have more of a lasting effect than anything else.

Needless to say, we could not wait to get paid. Having a job on the streets has its downfalls though. Every one of our homeless friends knew that we were getting paid soon and would not stop bugging us to buy them clothes, food, and beer. Carrying that much cash was dangerous, so we only let a few people know when we got paid.

Day 31

July 1 marked one month since my parents dropped me off. The time was still not exactly flying by, but it was Tuesday, which brought me one day closer to getting paid. Even though I was excited to receive my fortune, I didn't lose any sleep over it. I did, however, lose sleep over the Ambassadors waking me up at 4:30 in the morning. No worries though; we just moved to our backup spot just out of their jurisdiction. Or so we thought. We thought that we could get a few more hours of sleep hiding behind the animal statues. We had gotten away with it before, but not this time. For some reason, the Ambassadors were cleaning up the streets that day. Sleep deprived, we all made our way to Woodruff Park to play cards.

Despite waking up so early, I was actually having a good time. Playing cards took me back to my days at Leroy, my college dorm. Freshmen year was full of late-night card games that got so intense that the resident director would come to our room quite regularly to tell us to keep quiet. Fortunately, I was prepared to play spades on the street by the time I got there. They don't teach that in the classroom.

Mikey and I had a good four-player game of spades going with Josh and his new friend Nemo when Jimmy and Luna walked up. Josh and his new friend Nemo took off as soon as the drama-filled couple arrived. Jimmy said a few words and then walked away, leaving Mikey and me to finish our game of spades, so we decided to start a new two-player game.

Mikey began talking to me during the card game. He told me that his stepfather had just passed away. This is the stepfather that kicked him out of the house after getting out of jail, which led to Mikey being there on the streets. Mikey's sister sent him an e-mail telling him the news. His mother never even tried to contact him. Even though he was upset at his mother, he told me that he would try to call her that day, but he never did.

I enjoyed talking with Mikey because I could see so much good in him that wanted to shine through. I knew that goodness would not come without Christ. I could actually see a change taking place in Mikey. God was speaking to him, and I was blessed to see it. I encouraged Mikey before he headed off to work. He wanted to keep working, but I quit because that was not what I was there to do, and I hated the work.

After Mikey left, I saw a man digging in the trash for a meal, and I remembered the times a few days before when I had desperately searched the trash cans hoping to find something substantial. I was still in the habit of scanning each trash can I passed by to see if there was anything worth grabbing for later.

While I was in Romania helping run a summer camp for orphans, the bread that was left over from lunch was the bread that got eaten at dinner. That's not so uncommon, but when I had to stop one of the resourceful kids from pouring his leftover drink back into its original container to be used again, I tried to hide my laughter hoping that he would know that I was serious. I guess he was used to doing that where he is from. If I were back at the camp in Romania, I would have a hard time finding food from a trash can, but not so much in Atlanta.

I was carrying about five burritos that were given to me from a man at Buckhead Church the night before. When I saw the man digging in the trash, I was thrilled to be able to give him something good to eat. He was a little shocked, and his desperate digging rapidly came to a halt. His eyes got big and his dirty face lit up when he took the aluminum wrapper off. "IT'S BEEF!" he exclaimed. I guess he really liked beef.

While I was on the way to call my little brother Ezra on the phone for his birthday, I ran into another man digging in the trash for something to eat. I was again happy that I could give him one of the burritos. I loved eating them, but the joy and peace that came from giving them away was worth not having the security of knowing where my next meal would come from.

"Cease striving (be still) and know that I am God; I will be exalted among the nations, I will be exalted in the earth" (Psalms 46:10). As simple and effortless as it sounds, to be still is a very difficult task. In the world we live in, certain fast food restaurants will give you your order for free if it is not ready in a certain amount of time. High-speed Internet can't get fast enough. People in front of you don't drive fast enough. The person you are calling doesn't pick up the phone fast enough. To slow down is one thing, but to stop and be still is almost unheard of. The English word "still" is hard enough, but here are some other English words I like that are derived from Hebrew: "slacken," "cease," "slothful," and "(be) weak (-en)." I used to think that this verse was simple: do nothing and think about God. If we are still before God, we not only see His magnificence but also see just how small and weak we are.

Having nothing to do allowed me to slow down for a moment and stay there. It made it a little easier to be still. I have breathed fresh air, but not in downtown Atlanta. I have felt a cool breeze, but in Atlanta, the main breeze came from the busses, which were followed by an exhaust cloud. Not much natural beauty surrounded me, but for some reason I was content and loving every moment of being still.

I was sitting at a table in the park just after calling my brother. A lady's voice from across the street was filling the air with different Gospel songs. She was almost shouting and her voice sounded worn, but it was so beautiful there in that moment. I tried to relax and not think about what I was going to do next. I could feel God's presence stronger there than in any of the churches I had visited. A pigeon flew just above my head, and despite the noisy downtown streets, I could hear its wings flapping. I remember it as if it were in slow motion. The colors that I saw seemed brighter. The grass looked greener, and the sky looked brighter. I enjoyed the massive skyscrapers that made me feel small. All my senses seemed to wake up! It was amazing. When I was there at the table, distractions could not even take over. Jimmy came running up to me and felt the need to show me his stash of weed. Someone yelled at the lady across the street and she stopped singing, but that did not kill the presence of God. He is much more powerful and potent than any physical object could destroy.

Mikey returned after finding out he didn't have to work. It was a good thing, too, because God gave me the opportunity to talk to Mikey about the teachings of Christ. We talked about temptation and how God promises a way out. We talked about forgiveness and how he needed to forgive the guy who beat him up and put him in the hospital. After talking, he told me that he loved learning about the Bible. Praise God!

After a while, we decided to walk to the other end of the park to play chess. Before learning on the streets, my little sister always beat me at chess, so I still wasn't very good. There were six or seven chess tables, and all were full. Crowds of all sorts of people would gather around us, some looking to play the winner. Fortunately, Mikey was no better than I was, so I stayed at the table for the first couple rounds. John, Josh, and another friend whom we called Bootleg joined us. I was having a good time until the preaching started. Someone started shouting at other people about their sin. He was quite annoying because he sounded angry at the world instead of being full of love for people. I was trying to have a peaceful rest of the day, but this guy was pushing it. Everyone around me felt the same way.

Mikey and I talked a little about the character of God, but I guess we didn't cover the issue of drugs well enough. He was good at hiding things from me. I should have caught on when Mikey wanted to go do something with Josh and Nemo, but I didn't. We walked to a small parking deck and sat down to resume our four-player card game. As soon as we sat down in the corner of the parking deck, Josh started to roll up a joint. Mikey just stared at me wondering what my reaction would be. I knew he had a guilty conscience.

We started our game of Hearts as Josh lit up. He then passed it to Mikey who, after taking a puff, handed it to Nemo. I don't know how much Nemo had smoked before, but he took a puff of marijuana and almost gagged. I think that he had only been on the streets for a couple weeks. He passed it to me, and I passed it to Josh. "He don't smoke you little retard," Josh said to Nemo. "Don't pass it to him." It went around again, and Nemo gagged a little more and passed it to me. "What's wrong with you? I said he don't freakin' smoke," said Josh. Eventually Josh tried to get me to smoke, but after I told him no, he quit asking me. We finished our game and headed to Safehouse to eat, with three of us high and one of us sober. Seeing Mikey's and even Josh's reaction in regards to my character gave me an advantage in sharing Christ with them. It seemed hopeless most of the time, but these guys saw my lifestyle and compared it to theirs and I was able to see they wanted to be better because of me.

Our friend Bootleg decided to stay over at our place for the night. Bootleg came to Atlanta to land a record deal. According to him, he was a rapper trying to record an album. He moved there and quickly ran out of money and was on the streets. He always had a plan to make a million dollars, but until then, he asked Mikey and me when we were getting paid so we could buy him some food, but because of his size, it did not appear that food was his greatest need. He was rather large, so I tried to stay on his good side. We asked him to rap for us, which I soon regretted. He randomly spit out words, and if he couldn't think of anything else, he filled the void with the F-word.

I wasn't sure where Bootleg normally stayed, but it was actually nice to have a little change in company. He tried to figure out Mikey's jokes, which were funny because they were meaningless, so it was entertaining to watch Bootleg try to understand the meaning of a meaningless joke.

Day 32

Early Wednesday morning, we woke up to Ambassador horns once again, so we moved behind the animal statues. For the second time, we were woken up and told we could not stay there. We used to sleep there without much trouble, but for two days now we hadn't been able to. I found out that there was a gay pride parade going on later in the day and that was the reason we could not sleep past 5:30 a.m.

I was so sleepy and just wanted to lie down anywhere, but I found no rest. After getting breakfast at 7:00, I split off from Mikey, John, and Bootleg. I walked the streets desperately looking for a place to sleep. I could hide in bushes, but the bugs would eat me alive. Trust me, I know from experience. As big as downtown Atlanta is, there are so many people that fill it up and make it nearly impossible to find a place to sleep during the day.

I walked around Centennial Olympic Park and finally gave out on a bench. I remembered sitting down and taking out the cereal bar that was left from breakfast and eating it. A few minutes later, I awoke to a loud whistle in my ear. The not-so-friendly park police thought that blowing a whistle in my ear would be a nice thing to do. I didn't remember even laying down, but I was out cold on that stone bench. I'm normally okay with having nothing to do when I'm tired because I can normally go to sleep, but I was forced to stay awake with nothing to do and lacked the motivation to read or write.

The Atlanta Union Mission is a shelter I was planning on staying in that night. I was told that I needed to arrive there in the early afternoon to make sure that I would get a bed. To even think about a bed made my tired face smile. This would be the first shelter I had stayed in, and I was not all that excited about it. Yes, I would get a bed, but I would be at ground zero again when it came to knowing people or having friends to talk with.

Even though I was going to get a bed that night, I was still tired after being rudely awoken for the third time that day. In between the Georgia Dome and the Philips Arena, there is a large courtyard that is practically deserted when there are no events taking place. I was finally able to sleep there for a few minutes. I didn't want to get woken up again, so I left before anyone came.

Like I said before, in order to get a bed, you have to reserve a spot by being at the shelter in the early afternoon. I arrived at the Atlanta Union Mission at 3:00 p.m. and waited in line outside. A big advantage to being homeless was the freedom. Staying at a shelter temporarily takes away that freedom, which is why many homeless people avoid them. I waited in line for three and a half hours! Once again, I felt so alone and it was making me miserable.

Finally, 6:30 p.m. came, and I heard them announce that we would be able to check in. The line moved slowly, but at least it was moving. When I made it to the door, I checked my bag in and they put it in a locker. I was glad to see that they kept peoples' belongings locked away to avoid people bringing weapons or drugs.

I was then pointed down the hallway with no one telling me what to do next. The people that worked there did not seem very happy or helpful, but I just followed the crowd. I asked one guy who was staying there what to do: "Just keep to yourself and don't talk to anyone and you will get out okay." His words didn't exactly ease the doubts I had about staying the night.

I got to the end of the hallway where there was a man asking for my clothes. I then I realized, as he gave me a small bar of soap, that everyone who stayed there had to take a shower. I stripped down and walked into the large shower searching for an open shower head, as if I wasn't uncomfortable enough. After finding an empty shower head in the crowded shower, I let the hot water rinse the dirt off of me. I felt like a new man. I knew that I would have to put my dirty clothes on after I got out of the shower, so I tried to savor the clean feeling for as long as I could.

Once I got out of the shower, I was given a T-shirt to dry off with. Water was still dripping off my face as I was directed up the stairs to my room. When I saw the room that I was going to be sleeping in, it reminded me of the dorm rooms of some friends of mine in China. Bunk beds were placed with just enough room in between to squeeze into them.

About twenty minutes went by while I was lying on the bed before a man with a loud speaker came through the halls telling everyone to go downstairs for dinner. I was ready to eat, to say the least. Breakfast held me over until about 2:00 p.m., so by 7:30, I was ready to eat. One ten-ounce cup of soup and a piece of bread was all we had for dinner. I thought that there would be seconds, but when I asked, I found out that this was it. I still had a bed to look forward to, but first I had to sit through the preaching.

"I hope the preacher gets a flat tire and can't make it," one of the guys at my table said. I wondered how many people would stay for the preaching if they were given a choice. I wondered if I would stay if I were given a choice. The preacher presented the Gospel via a slideshow of cartoons. People were talking and laughing out loud while he was sharing, which I guess was typical there. The guy across from me was talking about a sandwich the entire sermon. His soup must not have hit the spot.

When the preacher got to the last slide, he asked everyone to be quiet. I thought to myself, oh, no; don't do it. "Repeat after me." He led the crowd in the sinner's prayer. Preachers often make salvation sound easy. Christ made it sound nearly impossible. If anyone wants to follow Christ, they must first disown themselves to make room for Christ to rule and, on top of that, carry their own cross (torture device; Matt 16:24 paraphrased). Jesus would also say things like, "If anyone comes to Me, and does not hate his own father and mother and wife and children and brothers and sisters, yes, and even his own life, he cannot be My disciple" (Luke 14:26) and "And Jesus said to him, 'The foxes have holes and the birds of the air have nests, but the Son of Man has nowhere to lay His head'" (Luke 9:58). And when one man wanted to follow Him but wanted to say good-bye to his friends first, Jesus said, "No one, after putting his hand to the plow and looking back, is fit for the kingdom of God." (Luke 9:62). I think you get the picture.

Jesus didn't say it's as easy as A-B-C. A—Admit you are a sinner, B—believe Jesus died on the cross for you, and C—confess your sins to God. I have heard this many times. There are many truths in this prayer, but making it sound easy to be a follower of Christ is damning! Many times the sinner's prayer diminishes the cost of true Christianity and attempts to give away "get out of hell" cards. The saddest part of all is that many times the cards are counterfeit; sometimes they're not given intentionally, but they are worthless because there was no real change in the sinner's heart. And the people receiving the tickets have no incentive in getting another because they already have one. But when the time comes, they will find out it was a fake. Let's not hand out fake passes by diminishing the cost of becoming a true follower of Christ.

After the preacher finished the prayer, he asked if those who repeated after him and meant it would raise their hand. I wasn't shocked to see half the people in the room raise their hand, but when the man across from me who talked about a sandwich the whole time raised his hand, I wondered how he even knew to because it didn't seem like he had been listening to anything. I wondered if those people believed that saying a few words saved them. If it was anything like Safehouse, those raising their hands weren't doing it for the first time.

Finally, I was allowed to go lie down in the bed I had waited hours for. I was looking forward to a great night of sleep, but I had to wait a few minutes in bed before it was time to cut the lights out. I listened to the other fifteen people in the small room talk about how to hustle. "Hey, man, how do you hustle people for money?" some would say. It was a little humorous because they were hustling each other. They were trying to trade candy and talk down to each other. Even though I learned how to hustle, I never put those skills to use. Some would give their opinion on which cardboard signs worked best, while others discussed how they manipulated people into giving them money.

The hustle discussion led to talk of drugs, which led to a drug deal. Here I was, sharing a small room with fifteen other grown men who were dealing drugs and trying to hustle each other before going to sleep. I was told when to eat, sleep, wake up, and bathe, and I was made to listen to a sermon, but I had a bed with a stained, holey sheet. Needless to say, staying in the shelter was not the best experience of my time on the streets. I also think that I was the only one not snoring that night, mainly because everyone else's snoring kept me awake. I would've thought that none of that would matter because I was used to a noisy street, but for some reason, I slept much better on the sidewalk. There was always a chance you'd be woken up at five in the morning on the streets, but you were certain to be awake by five in the shelter.

Day 33

After waking up at five the next morning, I brushed my teeth and waited in line for breakfast. Fortunately breakfast was much better than dinner, and I was able to eat a warm meal that filled me up.

There was a kind man there serving food. He was probably in his early thirties, and I think that he was also homeless, but he was volunteering. He had the same demeanor as Mrs. Kay, the breakfast lady, Mike the Catholic, and the young lady that talked with us at Safehouse. Those were the kinds of people that showed they care through simple little actions that proved their authenticity, and it did not take long at all for people to pick up on that. They would look me in the eye for more than a second, they would ask and remember my name, and they would talk with me as if that was where they genuinely wanted to be. Their authenticity was so real that I could not ignore it.

Anyway, as I was getting food, the man simply told me I was allowed to come back for seconds. I wished he had been there the night before. After eating my breakfast, I was more than ready to leave and see my friends. Little did I know that it was going to be another long night on the streets.

It was an exciting day! This was the day we could get our paychecks! After finding Mikey, we headed to the AmericasMart Atlanta building to pick up our checks. It was strange walking into a bank, though. I had been on the streets for a month, and that was plenty of time to feel like a homeless person. I felt like I was doing something wrong walking into a business. While we waited in line, I looked around to see if anyone was going to tell us to leave, but to my surprise, no one did.

We walked out of the bank with a lot of cash in our pockets. I felt rich! With $187, I was free to do whatever I wanted. Mikey had a little over $200, and the fun week was about to begin! I have to admit that I was a little scared to be carrying that much money while living downtown, so we didn't tell anyone except John. If we had any change, I was sure to secure it in a place that didn't make any noise otherwise people would know we had money. After getting the money, I split up from Mikey and John, which turned out to be a bad idea.

When I later found John and Mikey at Hurt Park, they were in the middle of sharing a joint. When they were done, one of their friends in the park asked them desperately for the roach. How sad it was to see a homeless man get so excited about getting even a tiny amount of the very thing that kept him in his current situation. Are we any different with our own sinful desires? His sin happened to be illegal, but when I make a habit of breaking God's law, am I any less pitiful?

By the time I found John and Mikey, it was time to head to Safehouse for dinner. "Okay, everyone stop talking so I can preach." The man from last week put a stop to the conversations going on so we could hear the same message that I, and many others there, had heard last night, and the night before, and so on.

Among the people that served the tea and donuts to us before the sermon were Adam and Mrs. Mary. After the sermon was over, everyone got in line for hot dogs. After people received their hot dog, they made their way to wherever they were sleeping that night. The sweetest, and I would say most effective, part of the night was just before the sermon when people like Adam and Mary talked with and took care of us. Adam was getting to know Mikey and asked him if he had been clean. I was waiting to hear Mikey's response because he was high at the time. I was glad to hear that Mikey told him the truth. In 2 Corinthians 8–9, Paul talks about how he boasted in the believers. It is so nice to be able to do that. In my journal I wrote, "Praise God for all the saints that are worth boasting about."

"Don't do that right here! Are you crazy?" After Safehouse, we went to Centennial Olympic Park where Mikey decided to change his shorts in front of a few hundred people. We had both talked about getting in the fountain at the park for a while, and here we were, but I didn't know that Mikey was going to drop his pants in front of everyone. Anyway, the water show was going on while we were there, and we couldn't get in until it was over, so Josh, John, Mikey, and I waited.

While we were on the way to the park, Mikey split off to get a fruit punch and some cigars for himself. It was super nice to have the ability to get our own drinks now, but I was a bit naive about the whole fruit punch thing. We could get what we wanted, when we wanted it. I call that luxury!

There were a lot of kids at the park and everything seemed fine—almost too fine—and then Mikey changed in front of everyone. No wonder he didn't think twice about changing in front of everyone: most of his punch was gin. My frustration with Mikey began when he was standing in the middle of the fountain with kids surrounding him, smoking a cigar. I took off after him to save him from trouble with security or police. That was the first sign that it was going to be one crazy night on the streets.

I didn't realize the punch was heavily spiked until I asked for some fruit punch when we were walking to the spot. Mikey didn't want to give it to me because he was trying to keep it a secret from me. He finally gave me the plastic fruit punch bottle and I took a sip. I just looked at Mikey and shook my head. The day he got paid, he used drugs and alcohol.

When we passed by the liquor store on the way to go sleep, Mikey wanted to buy us all sodas. How convenient that the store nearest to us to get something to drink was a liquor store. We left the store all carrying sodas except Mikey. Mikey bought another bottle of gin, although he tried to hide it from me at first.

John and I walked ahead of Mikey and Josh because he was starting to make a fool of himself from being drunk. He was talking to everyone on the street and stumbling around by the time we got back, which was only about a twenty-five-minute walk. I wanted Mikey to just lie down and go to sleep, but that would have meant that the night was coming to an end, and it was just beginning in his eyes! It was amazing to see how quickly he misused the money.

John and I tried to go to sleep, but I was worried that Mikey would start playing pranks on us, and there was no telling what Mikey would do. I wanted a restful night, so I warned him not to touch me. He and Josh were talking at the church when Mikey's friend James walked up. They decided to go back to the store and get more gin so they wouldn't run out. Finally, I could sleep because they were gone. A few minutes later Mikey came back freaking out because he lost his money. I was thinking to myself, this is great, now we can't go to Six Flags or do anything else we had planned because Mikey wasted and then lost all his money.

Mikey started roaming the streets looking for his money. He could walk, but not very well. I watched from the church doorstep as he asked people randomly on the streets where his money was. I knew that this could not end well, and John told me that we should move to the animal statues down the street because he didn't want Mikey to jeopardize us being kicked out of our spot at the church permanently. I took his advice because I knew there was nothing I could do for Mikey at this point.

I tried to get some sleep at the animal statues, but guess who showed up before I even got a chance. About an hour later I heard, "I love you man!" Mikey found us, and now he was telling us how much he loved us. He remembered where his money was as he was taking off his shoe and a hundred dollars fell on the sidewalk. The bills were going everywhere, but I was able to snatch them up before anyone else saw them. I couldn't tell whether Mikey liked me or hated me. He got in my face to tell me how much he cared about me, but he also started kicking me as well. I assumed he was simply playing around, but all I wanted was to sleep. I knew that he would fall asleep soon if he would simply lie down on the concrete. My attempts to get him to sleep were failing though.

It was down to the three of us: John, Mikey, and me. John was running low on patience, so he walked away. For some reason, I told him to take his time and that I would look after the drunk guy to make sure he didn't get himself killed. After a few more times of kicking me and telling me how much he loved me, Mikey finally settled down. Before he lay down, he took off his new clothes that he bought that day because he didn't want to get them dirty. So there I was in the part of town that I wanted to stay away from with Mikey, who was drunk and in his underwear.

He was nearly naked and laying on the concrete, and I had to do something. I remembered that he had been carrying a blanket with him, so I put that over him for cover. Even though he was drunk, he was smart enough to let me hold on to his money for the night. I thought he was safe once I saw that he was asleep. Before I could calm down enough to get any sleep myself, an angry lady came up looking for some jeans.

If I were a homeless person in need of some clothes, I would not go to other homeless people in the middle of the night to find them, but that's just me. I was caught off guard when I heard her loud voice. "You got any jeans?" she asked, throwing in a few colorful words. She was drawing attention to us because of how loud she was, which was the last thing I wanted. "I don't have any jeans, but whatever I have you are welcome to take," I replied. I tried to be polite and peaceful so she would calm down and hopefully leave. I opened my bag up and started pulling out what I had. I had an extra T-shirt and a pair of shorts. My shoes were in there with my journal and Bible. When my bag was empty and she didn't find what she was looking for, she grabbed my bag to look in it herself. She held all the clothes up to take a good look at them as if she was in a department store. It was strange, but I guess nothing should be considered out of the ordinary out there. After taking my T-shirt and cursing at me (for what, I don't know), she walked off. Mikey asked who it was, and when I told him he just went back to sleep.

I waited for John to get back so that I could have a break from babysitting, but instead of John, it was the angry lady who came back. "You got any shampoo?" she asked. Confused once again, my brain produced no words for a few seconds because I was processing what she asked for. Then Mikey woke up. "NO! We don't have no F-in' shampoo. Now go away."

I was sitting on the concrete and Mikey was a few feet away on the ground. The lady walked over to Mikey and they started going at it. "This is just great," I thought to myself. I had never fought before and I didn't want to start now, but I didn't leave the scene of this argument because I needed to protect Mikey. She was pushing him and was about to kick him, and frankly, she could have beat him in the state he was in. I don't recall getting up at all, but I remember that one moment I was sitting down and the next I was in the lady's face! I had forced myself in between them and my hands were wrapped tightly around her wrist. When I shoved her back away from Mikey, I stared at her with just about two inches between our faces and firmly said, "You do not want to do this! I'm cool with you, but it would be a good idea for you to leave!" I saw the fear in her eyes as she nodded in agreement. When I let go of her wrist, she took off.

I had not spoken to anyone like that before and have not since then, but it got the job done. I still don't know how I was so firm and rude. I thought that I might be okay now that the lady was gone, but she screamed from across the street, "I'm goin' to get my boyfriend and he's gonna kick your butt." So the question was, should I drag Mikey, who had already passed out again, around downtown, or should I wait there to see if she would bring her boyfriend? I decided to stay because it would have been impossible to safely move Mikey and his stuff to another location. I was also banking on the lady bluffing.

I was anxious for John to get back for many reasons. Maybe he would know what to do. The blanket that once covered Mikey's body was now laid beside his nearly naked body. To no surprise, he started to vomit all over the street. I dragged him out of the puddle, placed the blanket back on him, and put his new clothes on. When I did so, I found another fifth of gin that had not been opened yet. After throwing the bottle away, I tried to get some rest with no success.

By the time John got back, it had been a couple hours, so I didn't think that the lady even had a boyfriend. John advised us to go back to the church without Mikey and leave him his old clothes. I gladly took him up on the offer because I was certain that no one was going to return at that point. As I lay down on the sidewalk outside the church, I could not stop thinking about Mikey. I was praying for his safety, even though I knew that he had probably seen worse nights.

I guess it was around 3:00–4:00 a.m. when Mikey walked up and started kicking us again to wake us up. He cursed at us for leaving him but then told us how much he loved us once again. We got him to lie down, and he quickly fell asleep. Not long after Mikey's return, the Ambassadors made us leave. We were all so tired, so we found a little park and got about thirty more minutes of sleep before we were asked to leave by security.

Day 34

Mikey was still drunk, and he made it very difficult to go anywhere. I was under the assumption that Friday, July 4 was part of a long weekend for summer students. I thought that we would be safe to sleep at Hurt Park outside Georgia State University. We finally got there and lay down in the grass. Our plan was to leave Mikey there to sober up a bit and while we went to go eat somewhere. It was a long trip to the park because Mikey was talking to everyone on the street and wanted to go eat. It would have been easier to carry him if he were passed out.

It was great to have money to eat whenever we wanted to, so John and I went to the CNN building to buy some food and sit in the air conditioning. I loved being a paying customer because people couldn't kick us out. After eating and watching the news, we decided to head back to the park to check on Mikey.

"Your boy is in jail." Those were the words I heard from our friend Robert as we entered the park. The little hope I had left of us enjoying the next few days of luxury from my paycheck was instantly shot down. Apparently, it was not okay to sleep in the park that day even though there were no classes going on. The policeman woke Mikey up and told him that he could not sleep there. Mikey simply rolled over, but the policeman was persistent. Mikey finally got up, but when he did, I was told that he mumbled a few words about the policeman as he was walking away, and the policeman turned around and arrested him right there. I was planning on leaving in a little over a week, so I didn't even know if I would see him again.

John thought that I was going to be furious with Mikey for ruining our plans. Truthfully, I was angry and my patience was being stretched. I mean, how could Mikey do so well, start acting better around me, and then, as soon as he got a hold of some money, throw it all away within one day? To tell you the truth, nearly all the people that I met on the streets would have done the same thing. Mikey blew around a hundred dollars and was in jail in less than a day. That shows me what money can do in the hands of a homeless person. I am not saying never to give money to homeless people—I will get to that later on—but I am saying that we must be careful and discerning with what to give and to whom. I was upset with Mikey and disappointed, but God was teaching me to handle people who disappoint me with love and not anger.

I didn't plan on seeing Mikey anytime soon, so John and I started doing the things that regular people do, like eating out and watching movies. On the way to pick up an orange slush from the Varsity (a local fast food restaurant), we talked about our big plans that night. It was the fourth of July, so we tried to think of the best free firework show to go to. We decided that we would go to Centennial Olympic Park because it was the nearest to the spot.

Even though someone from a church that feeds us gave John twenty dollars every week, he rarely used that money on food, which was no surprise. I couldn't wait to go out to eat and watch a movie in a theater! I was excited to say the least. I am not sure if it was because I would feel closer to home by being somewhere that only people who paid money could be or if it was because I would feel more out of place for a change. Nonetheless, I was excited. We walked to Seventeenth Street and then over I-85 to Atlantic City—a development in midtown that was thriving. The apartments were expensive, and the stores were very nice. The cars that I saw and the people walking down the street were very different from just a few blocks down the road. I felt out of place because there were no other homeless people around. It was a slightly uncomfortable feeling, but as soon as we would get in the dark theater, no one would notice that we were out of place.

As I entered the theater, the smell of buttery popcorn hit me. John and I were living it up. Tickets were ten dollars each, so my money was also diminishing rapidly. I was lucky and blessed to be able to take a homeless man to a movie and to see him enjoy it. I was also able to make him feel comfortable enough around me so that I could see the real John. I knew who he was, and he didn't change that like he usually did in front of others. It took time to get to know him, but it was great to be able to do that for him.

Later when we got to Centennial Olympic Park, I felt out of place once again. Thousands of people had gathered to watch the show. There were families and people of all different ages. I didn't see any of my homeless friends there though, so it was just John and me. The firework show was spectacular, but one of the most exciting parts was when a firework went off a little too close to the ground. John had to put out a burning ember that landed on a girl's blanket next to us, but that was about the extent of our contact with the public while in the park.

Going from being in the middle of thousands of people and returning to the church doorway in downtown Atlanta made me feel alone and invisible. Once we were settled in our spot, there were still thousands of people everywhere. Hundreds walked by without even looking at us. After a while of people watching, our Catholic friend Mike came by with some of his friends. They had also been at the firework show. He not only gave us as much of their leftovers as we wanted, but also he made me feel visible again. He introduced us to all his friends, and they actually shook our hands. It was nice to meet normal people who were interested in meeting you through a friend and not out of guilt. They didn't stay long, but it was nice to have a group of people to talk to.

There was no way we could have thought about eating all the food Mike left with us because there was so much. After sharing with the other homeless people in the doorway and still having plenty, I told John that we should give some to the people across the street. He wanted nothing to do with that for some reason. He just said that I was in charge of the food and I could do it if I wanted to, but I would have to do it alone. I was a little shocked at his response because he usually helps others. John's blatant apathy for sharing with those in need surprised me. We had plenty, and we knew that there were others across the street that needed what we had been given, but he didn't care about helping them. John was full and wanted to relax in his comfort. We are commanded to take care of others in need as Christians, but some are often as blatantly apathetic about helping as John was. God gives gifts to us to enjoy but also so that we can give.

A couple of days before, Mikey had introduced me to his friend James. James was middle age, very kind, and completely honest: almost the opposite of how Mikey had been acting. I had seen James often since that night. He sort of moved in just as Mikey went to jail, so they kind of swapped places.

Day 35

I left John and walked with James to go get some of Ted's soup. I found out that James and I had a similar mind-set about the street life. We talked about why homeless people are treated the way they are. We agreed that most of the people on the streets thought that the world owed them something. James said that 90 percent of the people out there were jerks. That statement may or may not be true, but it was nice to hear something like that come out of the mouth of another homeless man. He said, "The people out there know where to go to get help, but they would rather stay out doing their own thing." It was encouraging to hear James say those words. He thought highly of people trying to help him and others like himself, while most of the homeless community complained about the help they received. James knew that the problem that kept him on the streets was his problem, and he admitted that.

At first, I thought that James was joking when he proudly said that he had been clean for two days. I later saw how that was a big deal to him, but at the time I didn't know. His addiction to crack was his downfall and the main reason he was living on the streets. It was not very often that I ran across someone with a positive outlook and a thirst for change, but James gave me hope. He was desperately trying to get started with a program to help him get back on his feet again. He knew of so many places where I should go to for help in getting myself off the streets. It was a little difficult to turn them down without him finding out my actual reason for being there.

After lunch at Ted's, James and I parted ways, but that was not my last encounter with James. I met back up with John and saw a tiny glimpse of his honest side. That moment didn't last long, but it was something. We were sitting down on a bench when he asked me out of the blue, "Do you think that someone could be too far gone and done too many bad things that God would not accept them?" I was excited that he opened up to me a bit, but as soon as he opened up, he shut back down. When I gave him the answer, he sarcastically mumbled "that's what he thought I would say." He didn't want to hear that someone would forgive him. I guess he wanted me to say, "No, John, God will not forgive you because you are too bad so you might as well just keep living a sinful life."

The question is, how can we reach people like John whose hearts are so hardened? I don't have the answer, but I do want to be encouraging. I spent an entire month with Mikey and John, and they were not the worst people on the streets to be with. In fact, they were some of the best. Mikey got a job and John volunteered almost every day, so there was improvement, but it was very little. After a month of trying to encourage them and make a change in their lives, Mikey was in jail and John did not want to hear anything I had to say. It appeared that my efforts were in vain, but my heart was full. Why was my heart full? By all means, I had failed in making a positive difference in anyone's life. The answer is obedience. In 1 John 2:3 it says, "By this we know that we have come to know Him, if we keep His commandments." I was being obedient to God, and I knew that anything else that happened around me in the lives of others was simply icing on the cake.

James made the statement that people on the streets know where to get help if they want it but that they would rather do their own thing. We need to ask ourselves if we are any different at all. As Christians, we know where to get help from for anything life gives us, but we often don't want God's help because we like our freedom.

Oddly enough, I met a couple of guys who were not homeless that would wait in a long line at the shelters and other places to get a meal and just hang out. Jay was one friend that ate at these places even though he had a home, but there was another man named Bill who talked to me a couple of times while I waited in line at a hot dog stand. Now Bill was not a Christian, but sometimes I wish that church people would act a bit more like Bill. Let me tell you why.

After having an early lunch with James and after my conversation with John, I decided to take some time to be alone and rest from listening to people's problems. My alone time did not last very long because I was interrupted by Bill. Bill knew my name, but that was about it. He genuinely wanted to help me, which put me in a strange position because he asked me questions and I never gave him a straight answer.

"I see something different in you. You are not like other people out here." Did Bill know I was a fake? I was a little worried I might be found out. He knew the other homeless people around me, and I didn't want everyone to know. I was able to avoid telling him everything, but he was trying to find out why I was out there so he could help me get off the streets. Before Bill told me about his experience, he insisted on taking me out to eat. I was honestly not hungry at that time, but he wouldn't take no for an answer.

He got me whatever I wanted from the Chinese restaurant. I even got to enjoy an ice-cold soda! After leaving the restaurant, Bill told me that he had been homeless less than a year ago. He did not become homeless due to drugs or careless living, however. He was not homeless because he wanted his freedom. He told me that his troubles were strictly financial, which was why he was only on the streets for only two weeks. Before long, he was able to get a job and get back on his feet. He opened his wallet to show off how many credit cards he was able to get; maybe those had been the source of his downfall in the past. Nonetheless, he cared for me in a way that others did not. He did not wish me luck after buying my meal. He did not try to give me encouraging words without making sure I was full. I see three different avenues to care for a person: caring for their body, their soul, and their mind. Bill did well to care for my body; he made sure I did not go hungry. He also cared about my mental and emotional state. Like I said, he did not buy my food and leave. He spent time trying to help me get my feet on the ground. He looked at me when he talked to me. I could tell that he was not thinking about what he was going to be doing next. Bill was living in the moment. I understand that we are busy and do not have hours to spend with others, but we must ask ourselves what are we doing with the leftover hours we do have? I hope and pray that we are making an eternal difference somewhere.

Before we left each other, Bill offered for me to come to his apartment to get cleaned up and enjoy the air conditioning. I politely refused, but he let me know I was welcome any time. Even though Bill bought me a meal, spent time with me, and offered his home, he did not share the Gospel. I think that point is obvious: he was not Christian. The point I want to make is that, although Bill's intentions were different from a Christian's, his effectiveness in serving others is something Christians could learn from.

All throughout the scripture, we are instructed to serve one another in love. If others are not seeing the service as an act of love, then I fear that it is in vain. We must serve others in order to be obedient, but the second greatest commandment is to love others. If we skip the love part and go straight to serving others, then we will find ourselves weary and tired. May we love others and prove it to them by serving and genuinely caring for them.

Chapter 9

John Is Gone

Day 36

John had been a member of a Catholic church, and on Sunday of my last week on the streets, John and I decided to attend services at the church where we slept. The guard that usually woke us each morning was standing in the doorway where we had awoken a few hours earlier. It felt very strange walking by him to go into the church. I wasn't sure if he would try to stop us, but when we walked past, he didn't say a word. There were people in front of us walking through the foyer. Two ladies were handing out bulletins to people and greeting them with a smile and a "hello." When it was our turn, the lady's tone of voice changed. She said hello as if she was asking a question, you know, the kind of hello that means, "Can I help you?" Her smile also disappeared, but we kept walking through, and she never passed us a bulletin. I can understand her hesitation to a certain extent, but I was a little taken back by her reaction. I did get a smile out of someone during the service though.

My curiosity about how members would react to us kept me there until the service was over, but John left early. I'm honestly not sure why, but I stuck around. I saw a baby whose head was popping over her mother's shoulder a couple a rows in front of me. If you can't guess by now, that's where the smile came from. She kept looking right at me, which at this point was rare for anyone. I kept grinning at her, and she would smile back. Unfortunately, the service was over, and I received no more smiles. While I was walking out, there were people everywhere, and most of them were trying to shake hands with the priests. There were two priests standing on the sidewalk that I called home. They were trying to talk to everyone, or so I thought. I waited awhile for most of the people to clear. Just as they had a break, I walked by them. They were standing so close to each other that their robes were touching. I didn't see anyone walk between them because there was no room. I decided to make room. I tried to make eye contact with them, but even though there were no more people around, our eyes never met, nor did our hands. I walked right through the middle of them, which forced them to move over a bit, but they never said a word.

Later that day, I took John to go see another movie and then out to eat. John said that I was the most peculiar person he had ever met. I wasn't sure if I should take that as a compliment or not because I knew John had very peculiar friends. When I split up from John, I saw Jay, who was walking around downtown trying to give a cake to John because he knew that John was trying to leave town. Jay was the guy who lived with his parents but ate in the shelters with us. We'll get to that later. Jay also brought three items for me as well. He knew that I liked peanut butter, so he brought me a small jar and a shirt. I guess he thought I needed one, but I thought mine was fine. The last item he brought was a sleeping mask. I think he had seen me using my hat to cover my eyes. He finally found John, and we all ate the cake he had made. John was close to tears because Jay's kindness.

I was hoping to see Mikey soon, but I had no clue if I would. After falling asleep that Sunday night, a man walked up in the middle of the night and just started talking to us. I guess it was better than the night before when I woke up and found that our spot in the doorway was a bit more crowded because someone had fallen asleep right between John and me. This man, who I could see through the tiny hole in my hat, was cursing at us and telling us how sorry we were. I thought to myself, it's the middle of the night and you have nothing better to do than to curse at homeless people while they sleep. I was cautious whenever someone would do things like that, but after he told us he was walking home 150 miles away, I had no trouble going back to sleep.

By this time, I was able to sleep through a lot, which had its ups and downs. The upside was that my body could actually rest despite the noise of traffic, sirens, and people. The downside was that anyone could come up and I might not even know it. Another downside was that I could wake up too late in a rain storm and already be soaked, which was exactly what happened that night. I thought I was sleeping hard, but I had to wake up John so he could get out of the rain too. Once again, I hugged the door of the church trying to keep as dry as I could for the night.

Day 37

If you'll recall, John couldn't get a job at Kroger because of his warrants in St. Louis. From what I understood, John had serve time in jail for a few months in St. Louis. The only problem was that the warrants were misdemeanors, and the police office in Atlanta would not take him or send him to St. Louis. John was stuck in Atlanta and was unable to get a job. He was trying to go to jail, but he couldn't even get there. I'm not sure if all this was true, but Jay and I wanted to help John as much as we could.

John said that he was going to go to Traveler's Aid to see if they would help him. This social service agency provides a variety of services to homeless people, including transportation. John, however, was not so eager to return to St. Louis. To this day, I am not sure how true his stories about needing to go to jail in St. Louis were, but Jay and I wanted to at least try getting him to St. Louis. Every chance John got to postpone the visit to Traveler's Aid, he took it. Monday morning, the three of us went down to the Traveler's Aid office, but as soon as we got there, John wanted to use the bathroom. I know those were childish excuses, but this was what I dealt with 24/7. He wanted to go to another building to use the restroom, so I told him I would wait there on the street for him. I wanted to make sure he went through with it.

After a long visit to the library, which included checking e-mail as well as using the restroom, John finally made it back to the office. We all went in, and John waited to talk to the lady at the desk. Unfortunately, there was nothing they could do. We spent half a day getting John to the Traveler's Aid office only to find out they couldn't help. It was at this time that I knew what I needed to do with the left over money that I had from my paycheck.

I spoke with Drew at Safehouse to see if we could find out where Mikey was, but we didn't have any luck. I wasn't even sure what his real name was. I needed Mikey around to keep me sane from being with John for too long. Mikey had his issues, but he could at least smile and joke around, which would brighten my day.

Later that afternoon I met back up with James and found him reading a Bible. This was a surprising scene for me, one that I had not yet encountered on the streets. I took a seat next to James on the sidewalk and asked him what he was reading. He told me that he was reading though Matthew and that he believed the Bible to be true. I am not sure what James' background was, but he seemed genuinely interested in what the Bible had to say. He told me that he was unworthy of what God had to offer. I explained that no one is worthy and told him that I would love to talk more about it the next day. I hated leaving, but I needed to make it up to Buckhead Church for my last Monday night service with the small group of friends I had made there.

A couple hours before talking with James, I found a "Breeze Card" lying on the street. This was different from the paper ticket you get for a one-time ride on the MARTA. I figured that there was nothing left on it, but when I checked, I found that it had unlimited rides until July 15! Even though I did love the four-hour walk to church, I was thankful to be able to ride the MARTA.

After my last small group session, some of my friends went out to eat and invited me to join them. I was enjoying their company so much that I didn't hesitate. I needed a break from the past few days, and spending another hour with believers was so encouraging. They gave me a couple of Gatorades, and one of the guys drove me home. The car ride was nice compared to the MARTA and much better than walking back in the dark. He dropped me off about a block away and I walked back to the spot, where I found John hanging out. James was off finding water. I fell asleep before he got back, but I left a Gatorade out for him. That night I slept like a baby until we were woken up by someone cursing at us, which wasn't very different from any other day. This time, however, I recognized the voice: Mikey was back! I was excited to see him, even though the last time I saw him he wasn't very pleasant to be around. He kept shouting, "I'm back! I'm back!" He asked us why we didn't keep him out of jail, while he kicked our legs. It wasn't long until we were up and tried to explain everything. I told him about how he had taken off his clothes and thrown up on the street. I told him about the lady that almost knocked him out. I did not, however, tell him that I threw an unopened bottle of gin in the trash. It was good to see Mikey because I was getting stressed out with John at my side all the time.

Day 38

Mikey told us that he had to go uptown to get his bags. Mikey, John, and I started our two-hour walk around 6:00 a.m., and when we got to the address, Mikey found out that his bags were somewhere else. Of course this did not go over so well with Mikey, but there was nothing else we could do about it. I let Mikey use my MARTA card to go to the correct address and meet us back at a nearby McDonald's. Keep in mind that we are about two hours from downtown, which made it even more difficult to find each other. So here I was, stuck with John again by myself. This was one point where I remember wanting it all to be over. I was tired physically, but I was even more tired mentally and spiritually. I knew that the end was near, which I'm sure didn't help my eagerness either, but I simply pushed through one hour at a time.

While in McDonald's, we decided to get a couple of biscuits with the money I had. On the way to get Mikey's bags, we told him that John was leaving Atlanta by bus later that day, and Mikey agreed to pay part of it, which allowed me to spend a few bucks on a meal. John and I were in McDonald's eating and killing time while we waited for Mikey when another homeless man came up to beg for some food. He had been there before, and the manager told him to leave. I walked up the register and asked if I could buy him a sausage biscuit off the dollar menu, but the man actually preferred a chicken biscuit. I couldn't believe it. I looked at him and said that I would get him something off the dollar menu, but he wanted to be picky. It didn't matter anyway because the manager told me not to get him anything. The man walked out cursing at the store and at me. Unfortunately, this attitude was common, and only a few of the people I was able to help genuinely appreciated it.

After two hours of waiting for Mikey, we decided to walk to the library now that we were full. Mikey ended up finding us at the library and, even though he told me he would not get drunk again because of the consequences, he was already drunk and high. I knew I should not have let him split up from us when he had his money. I was hoping that Mikey's return would be refreshing, but it was quite the opposite. At least with Mikey, I can tell him how I feel and he doesn't make up any excuses like John. While sitting at a table in Woodruff Park, I told Mikey how upset I was with him. He apologized to me, but I was not sure how long Mikey would last.

We weren't able to make it to Safehouse that night because John was leaving town that day. The ticket would cost eighty dollars, and the bus was departing at 6:30. I know I've said repeatedly that I was tired of John, and I was—I did not want to spend every hour of every day with him—but I must say it was harder than I thought to watch him go. James, Mikey, and I walked with John to the bus station. The walk wasn't far, but it did seem to take a while. We talked about the many memories we had made. We laughed at the stories of Mikey staring at people walking by and how fun Mikey's birthday party was. We walked slowly and joked a lot. Mikey was a bit more sober at this time, and James was also there to help keep me sane.

Once we made it to the bus station, I was a bit surprised to see John actually get on the bus. Before he got on, we gave him some cash and he looked back at us. He came up to me and kept saying how much he was going to miss me. His eyes were full of tears that ran all the way down his face. This moment was bittersweet for both of us. I hated that he had to go to jail, and I hated that he might not have someone to have a positive impact on him like I did. John knew the message of the Gospel; he had probably heard it more than you or I have. When I talked about it with him, he shut down, but I hoped that he would meet a good friend in St. Louis. That was the bitter side of things, but I knew that his leaving would be a weight off my shoulders. At that moment, though, I was only thinking about missing him. John walked onto the bus and sat at a window where he could still see us. He watched us until his bus drove away.

James came into the scene just as Mikey went to jail, and when Mikey returned, John was gone a day later. The doorway would still have three tenants, and I would still have two friends to help keep me sane for a few more days.

When we made it back to the spot, Jay was there and told us that he was planning on staying the night with us. I thought to myself how stupid that sounded. Why would someone who has a bed in a home ever stay out here on the sidewalk? That thought did not last long before I realized that I had done the exact same thing. We were excited to have him with us, and I was curious to see how he would handle sleeping on the streets for the first time.

Part of being homeless is losing pride. I may not have felt a loss of pride as much as most, but even sitting on the ground next to other homeless people while regular people looked on as they walked by was a humbling experience. Lying on the ground was even harder, but there was a way to maintain a little pride while sleeping on the streets: instead of getting as comfortable as possible in the doorway, Jay sat up in the corner and tried to lie his head against the door. I called it the "back killer," and it simply does not work. I had tried myself one night, but by that point, whatever pride I had when I first started my journey was gone. Sacrificing pride for comfort was a must if you wanted to survive. I curled up on the sidewalk, using my shoes for a pillow as if I was in my own bedroom. There were three doorways at the church, and Jay and I got the large one in middle while Mikey and James each got a smaller one.

Day 39

"Eli! Hey, man, let's get up." Jay woke me up and said that we should start walking. I searched for a glimpse of the sun but found nothing. The only light was from the streetlight. I knew that Jay had a phone, and even though he couldn't make calls, it did tell time. I asked him what time it was. "It's 3:00. We should start moving," he whispered again. I knew how he felt. I'm sure he hadn't slept much at all, and I remembered how I couldn't wait for the sun to come up my first few nights out here just to escape the misery of the night. I had no pity at that moment, though, because all I wanted to do was close my eyes and sleep. I advised him to lie all the way down and go back to sleep. I don't think that he ever went back to sleep, but I wasn't wasting the best two or three hours of sleep I would get that night.

I woke up earlier than usual because Jay kept waking me up. After I couldn't fall back asleep anymore, I decided to give in and just go to McDonald's with him. Nearly every night there was some issue getting me up earlier than I needed to be. Needless to say, I still did not feel well rested. Jay told me that some guy was shouting at us last night, but I did not remember any of it. There was no telling how many others came up to us while were sleeping.

Jay ordered off the dollar menu, but I was going to try to get some food and a hug from Mrs. Kay across the street. I was leaving the next day, which I was ready to do, but I knew that if I had no choice other than to be homeless, I would be able make it. I'm not sure if that was a comforting feeling or a scary one, but I was amazed at how quickly I acclimated to sleeping on the sidewalk every night.

I waited on the steps for Mrs. Kay with about fifteen other homeless people, but when she arrived, the only thing she had was hugs for all of us. This was the last one I received from her. I didn't get to know her as well as some of the other people, but she expressed her love to me and my friends as if we knew had known us for a long time. The funny thing was these homeless people that waited for her at least an hour every morning loved her back. You would think that they would have been mad and hateful about not getting any food, but they weren't. They just talked about how nice it was that she brought food to them at all.

We went to sit down near the church when someone jumped around the corner and shouted, "Give me all your money!" Our Catholic friend, Mike, scared us so much that I was speechless. Mike was just out and about and decided to sit and talk with us for a while. It wasn't long, but just a few minutes here and there made me and my other homeless friends feel visible. Mike was another person I knew I might not ever see again, but I couldn't tell him good-bye, so I just shook hands and said see you later.

Everyone split up to do their own thing, but all I could think about doing was sleeping. Like I said before, sleeping during the day was almost impossible. Every nook and cranny within miles was either guarded or too dangerous. I decided to take my chances at Centennial Olympic Park this time. I had slept there before and the police made me leave, but I wanted to try again. This time I tried to blend in with normal people. I sat in the grass close to some other people having a picnic. I loved how soft the grass was. It wasn't long before I was dreaming. It was a nice spot under a tree without my friends trying to wake me and no police were in sight. I could have stayed under that tree in the soft grass all day.

After getting a decent nap, I found James by himself and finally had a chance to talk with him about the Bible. I walked up to him and asked him if he had a chance to read more. He said that he read a little bit of Matthew yesterday, and when I asked him which chapters, he said all of them. I was shocked but encouraged at his interest in the Gospel. I explained to him that no one is worthy, and that was the point of the Gospel and the reason that Jesus came to die. James did not accept Christ that day, but I could tell the Holy Spirit was working on him in a powerful way. James reminded me a little bit of Bill. James told me that I should get involved in a program he was starting. He went to church almost every day, and the people were already helping him get back on his feet. James had no clue that by tomorrow night I would be taking a warm shower at home and sleeping in my own bed.

My last night on the streets was just like any other night. I got to the spot early to reserve it after eating at Safehouse. I felt homeless for sure by this point. I had no worries about going to sleep on the streets or going to shelters to eat. I wasn't worried about not being able to fall asleep either. My worries at that time were being arrested for sleeping in a park or going into a restaurant. I was worried about doing things that normal people would never worry about, like using the restroom in a restaurant or asking a businessman what time it was. I can't say that I wasn't excited that night though. I knew it was the last time I would use my smelly shoes as a pillow.

I was excited but also sad. I didn't know what to expect at all. I would miss my friends on the streets, and I would worry about them when I was gone. I wanted the people I was with to change, but I worried they wouldn't. I spent weeks with them with little to no improvement in their character. I'm glad it wasn't my job to change people, otherwise I would have failed. In 1 Samuel 15:22, it says that it is better to have obedience than sacrifice. I found that to be a very good truth. I was obedient in sacrificing my daily luxuries, but now that time had come to an end. My excitement didn't keep me up, though. I fell asleep one last time in the doorway of the church—the spot.

Back when I was first introduced to John, I met a few guys who were making a documentary called *My Concrete Mattress*. This documentary was intended to show that homeless people are not just a statistic but people with names and stories. These guys were planning on screening the documentary for the first time at a theater in Dublin, Georgia (a few hours south of Atlanta). The premiere was on Friday, July 11. John was featured in this documentary, and I planned on going with my friends from Buckhead. I had their phone number in my journal, and I planned on calling them the day before so I could join them on their trip to central Georgia.

Day 40

I was a few hours away from meeting up with my friends for a nice mattress and a full night's rest before waking up early to head to Dublin. However, I did have one more stop to make before I left. I split up from Mikey and walked to City of Refuge where my parents had dropped me off what seemed like ages ago. I was excited to talk with the people there and thank them for everything they had done. I had a couple of books and my huge backpack that I needed to get as well. Lindsey, who dropped me off downtown the first time in Five Points, took me the same route once again on our way back downtown, but this time it felt much different.

As I was riding in the front seat, I looked out of the window at what I had come to call home for the past six weeks. Inside the car, I could not smell the food being cooked and I could not hear the noise of all the people everywhere. When she had dropped me off the first time, I hadn't wanted her to stop—I could have ridden around for hours—but this time was much different. Things move slower while on the streets, which could be a pain, but at least I could take the time to look at people. This time I couldn't wait to get out of the car. She dropped me off at the same place as before, but this time I had no fear. Why was there fear the first time? Because everything was unfamiliar to me and I didn't know where to go. This time I knew what I was doing. God sometimes wants us to go to unfamiliar places, but our fear keeps us away. The only way to get over fear is to face it head on. I could have stayed in the car the first time and asked her to take me back, but that was not what God wanted for me. I could have slept in my own bed and spent time with my family all summer, but that was not what God wanted. I could have saved money, but that was also not what God wanted. Sometimes we, as Christians, live in fear of the unknown. But we must face our fears or never think about them again and continue to live life as a "good person" who never does anything radical.

I stepped out of the car with ease and made my way to Woodruff Park, where Mikey was sitting at a table. It had been nice not having plans for six weeks. I could sit and wait on someone for two hours and not think I was wasting time. Mikey and I started a game of chess, and the feeling of being there living in the moment was great. I knew what was coming next, but that was still a few hours away. At that moment, I was playing chess with Mikey.

It started getting late, so we headed up to Safehouse one last time. I saw James and Jay there for a minute before Bethany came to get me. Everyone was about to start piling into Safehouse, but Mikey and I walked up the street a bit. I left it up to Mikey to tell everyone else my story. I told him when I left that I would be back in a couple of weeks to see how things were and that I might even stay a night or two on the streets with him. After saying good-bye, I got into Bethany's car and she drove me to meet my friends from Buckhead.

My life on the streets ended as quickly as it began. The moment I stepped into Bethany's car, I knew that I would not be roaming around looking for food all day or waiting in line to spend fifteen minutes on a computer. I instantly felt distant from everyone around me, even though I had spent time with them before. None of them knew what it was like to be on the streets, and for some reason, it was difficult to connect with people off the streets. Bethany met up with my friends from Buckhead, where I stayed the night. A lot of friends were at their apartment, and they were all excited about going to Dublin the next morning. While everyone was inside, I stayed outside for a while and talked to my mom on the phone. It was difficult to put my feelings into words. I told my mom where we would be in Dublin, and my family was going to meet me there to take me home. The excitement I had about going home had gone away for some strange reason. I didn't want to stay on the streets, but for some reason I didn't feel comfortable sitting inside and having a good time with the other people. I thought about what Mikey was doing. He was probably at the spot by that time, and who knew where John was.

I thought about all my friends on the streets, but I soon became very sleepy. I knew that I had a bed in a room to myself, but I wondered how I would sleep. I wondered if I would wake up and want the heated sidewalk. In the six weeks that I was there, I had taken three showers. They were all community showers with a dozen other homeless men. For the first time in forty days, I was able to enjoy a private shower! It was glorious! I used so much soap and stayed in the shower for a while just letting the hot water wash over me. The best part of the shower was that I had clean clothes to put on afterward. Most of the time I was out on the streets, I didn't even know how bad I smelled. I knew that I didn't smell good, but I never thought much about it until I had to take a shower and put my nasty, sweaty clothes back on. This time was much different, however. I borrowed some clothes while my friends washed the clothes I had been wearing. When I got out of the shower and dried off, I went straight to bed. I was exhausted, but, to be honest, I wasn't sure what I wanted. I was torn between the street life and life at home. By no means did I have a desire to go back on the streets, but I knew that being away would be difficult; it was my new comfort zone.

I couldn't help but continue to wonder how I would sleep. The room was dark with no streetlight shining on me. I did not need my hat to cover my eyes. I was not worried about people trying to talk to me while I was sleeping or shoot at me with paint balls. I had blankets and a soft bed. I thought it was strange that the next thing I remembered was waking up the next morning. Come to find out, I did not need the traffic and sirens to put me to sleep. I had no problems whatsoever adjusting to sleeping in a bed again!

Day 41

When we got to Dublin, I felt like I was in a dream and that I would wake up on a bench somewhere. The air felt so cold inside because my body had acclimated to the heat. I hadn't spent more than an hour or so inside for weeks. My body changed after a few days of being out there, and it took a week or two for it to readjust back to normal. I could not believe how cold I was inside! I had a longing to be outside, not just because it was above seventy-five degrees, but because I did not feel comfortable inside. I was in the theater while they were setting up, and I had to get out! I went on a walk by myself nearby. I couldn't help but search for a good spot to sleep. I thought to myself, "That would be a perfect spot behind that big air-conditioning unit." I glanced at the top of trash cans every time I walked by to see if there was anything worth saving. I started to pick up a half-used cigarette for John. See what I mean when I said I felt and thought like a homeless person? I couldn't get away from it.

I walked back into the theater where they started up a sound check. I saw the video of John and my heart started breaking. I could not hold back the tears when I saw him on the screen. I was wearing the exact sweater he had on in the film because he had given it to me one night when I was cold. As much of a pain as John could be, I still cared about him. I knew that he didn't have a family coming to pick him up off the streets, and I knew that he didn't even have any friends with a car. Sure, John could have done better for himself, but he didn't have the luxuries in life that I did. I was trying to talk to one of my friends in the theater, but the only words I could get out were, "He is still out there."

My family was one of the first to arrive at the theater. I missed them, and when I hugged my mom, I just cried. I remember telling her as I hugged her that not everyone has this. Not everyone has a family that cares for them. Not everyone has friends who will spend time with them. There are too many people in the world that need a family. We as Christians should try to be their family.

Chapter 10

One More Night on the Street

By the time I got back home and started staying inside a lot more, my body had not adjusted to the luxuries around me. I tried to enjoy the conveniences that now surrounded me, but I was burdened for my friends on the streets. I would think about getting John and Mikey and bringing them back home. I could try to help them get a good job and let them get their feet back on the ground. The fall semester was about start, and I knew that bringing them home was not possible. But I still could not help but think about where they were and what they were doing. I knew then that I wanted to go back to Atlanta to see them, even if it was just for one night.

Two weeks went by when I drove my car to Atlanta to see Mikey and the others. Of course I knew I would not see John because he was likely serving his time in St. Louis, but I still just wanted to go back out to the place that had become home to me.

I drove straight to Safehouse, and Mikey was expecting me because we had been communicating via Facebook. I took Mikey out for fast food instead of eating at Safehouse that night. After we ate, Mikey showed me his new spot. He was now living in an abandoned hotel. It was an eleven-story building near Safehouse. It was already dark by the time we came in, and as we walked through the parking garage, there were homeless people on all three levels. I already felt uncomfortable. It wasn't nearly as bad as the first day on the streets, but I had my wallet with me this time. No one else knew, but it still made me cautious.

In order to get in, we had to jump from the third level of the parking garage to the roof of the lobby. From there we climbed onto one of the balconies. After we made it inside this abandoned hotel, Mikey gave me the tour. The place was gutted and reminded me more of a warehouse. Ivy grew out of the remains of a fountain, and the pool looked more like a swamp. Mikey walked behind me as we took the pitch-black staircase up to the seventh floor. A figure started walking toward me, but I said nothing. There weren't any other homeless people in the building that I knew of, but as I got closer, I could see that it was just Sherlock. Sherlock was a strange man, and he always had a strange woman with him. I knew him from Safehouse, but we never really saw him much, so I was curious how Mikey had started hanging out with him. Josh showed up, and when he got close enough to see that it was me, he ran up and gave me a huge hug! By this point, Mikey had told them my story, and they all thought it was pretty cool. They told me that the only other person ever to see where they lived were the people who made the documentary a few months ago. There was only one other person in the hotel, and that was Luna, Sherlock's girlfriend. I knew Luna because she was also Josh's girlfriend at one time, as well the fiancé of another guy just weeks before dating John.

Now it was time to see the whole place. Each floor looked exactly the same, but we finally made it all the way to the top floor. Sherlock led us through the top floor and then pointed up. The ladder that hung down from a small shaft dangled about four feet from the floor. Josh helped all of us up before coming up the ladder himself. The street from this point of view was much different. We could see Safehouse just one block away. Instead of feeling like there were people all around us, as we did when we were sleeping in the doorway, we felt like the world was far below and that we were out of danger. This spot seemed quite nicer than the doorway, but it wasn't necessarily safe. Like I said before, it was much safer in the day than it was in the dark.

That night, Mikey and I slept on a balcony on the seventh floor of what used to be a hotel room. There was shelter over our heads, but I couldn't sleep much. I kept worrying about my wallet for some reason. I had money when I was on the streets a few weeks ago, but this time I felt like a visitor.

When we woke up, I checked my phone for the time. It was nearly 9:00 a.m.! It was nice not having an Ambassador wake us up. I couldn't believe that it was even possible to sleep that late on the streets. After talking with Mikey about the past two weeks, he said he was doing well but that not much had really changed. He had no desire to get a job or live the way he knew he should. I didn't stay long, and after taking Mikey out for breakfast, I spent a few more hours with him before heading home. We looked for James but never found him. I told Mikey to stay in touch one last time and then I drove away.

After one semester of school went by, I came back to the streets. This time I found John back in Atlanta. Mikey had moved on by that point, so I wasn't able to see him. I met up with John and Jay in December that same year. John was used to staying at the spot, but I wasn't fond of freezing, so I suggested that we sleep in my car. We drove to Jay's apartment, where his brothers and cousins were everywhere in the small two-bedroom apartment. I finally understood why Jay stayed out there with us all the time. There was hardly any room to walk around in the place. After taking them out to eat, we went back to Jay's apartment where we could park the car and sleep. Throughout the night, I would crank the car to stay warm. I couldn't imagine sleeping outside in this weather every night. In the morning when I woke up, I asked John how he did it. He looked at me and just said, "I have no other choice." I knew what the answer would be, but when he said it, I felt bad for even asking. I remember him saying those words like it was yesterday.

Conclusion

The big question is "Why?" Why did I decide live on the streets? People always say that hindsight is 20/20, and that statement holds true here as well. What led me to begin my journey is explained in greater detail at the start of the book, but God used this experience to mold me into the person that he wanted me to become. We might not ever understand why God asks us to do something, but who are we to ask God to explain Himself? We are told to obey His commands, not to understand the ins and outs of His reasoning. We are to be obedient to His calling without question, and that is why I went: to obey God.

Now, I can see from an insider's perspective how homeless people are treated by society and the church. God used my obedience to mold me, but he is also using it to teach me how to effectively serve the homeless people around us, and I can now give insight on what to do and what not to do. Each person has a story!

Another big question I get is, "How?" How should we be serving not only the homeless but all people in need of a Savior? I wish that I could tell you exactly what to do when you're approached by a homeless person, but I can't. I have often heard people say to never give them money because they will just use it for drugs or booze. And while that might be true in most cases, think about how often we misuse the gifts that God has given to us. For example, whenever you come across a bit more time or money, is the first thought that enters your head, "What can I do with this gift to further the kingdom?" or is it, "What can I get to satisfy my desire for possessions?" I'm not telling you to always give money to the homeless. In fact, I would probably never do that myself. The best advice you could give them is to point them in the right direction. Learn what organizations in your town provide assistance to the homeless and tell them where they can go to seek help. If you start telling them where they can find a meal or a program to help them, they will more than likely leave because they already know where they can get help, and that is not what they want. Earlier I stated that the people on the streets that do not beg are the ones that help themselves. Keep this in mind and pray for discernment because it is a case-by-case basis.

If possible, you could even buy them a meal. Sometimes it's not possible because the restaurant won't allow it, which is what happened to me at McDonald's that one time. If they are truly hungry, you will be able to tell. Just like when I saw the guy digging through the trash can when I had leftover burritos. He was so excited and he started eating immediately. If you pass by the same homeless people frequently, by all means, get to know them. Learn where they come from and what they like. Sit on the ground with them. Mike and Mrs. Kay provide good examples of how to interact with the homeless. They wanted to help us, and we knew they wanted to because they cared about our lives. If your church feeds homeless people, make sure you let them know that you are not simply trying to pat yourself on the back. Remember their names, shake their hands, and ask them how their lives are, just like some of the people did at Safehouse.

These three examples are some of the best advice I can give for responding to the homeless: learn where they can get help, buy them a meal instead of giving money, and spend time with them. Whenever you are the one approaching them, or if you are already in charge of a homeless ministry, there are three main points that I found effective having been on the receiving end: minister to their bodies, their souls, and their minds.

There are resources needed to serve each of these aspects. To serve the body, we must have physical means. It costs money to give to the needs of one's body. Food can be donated without the use of money, but somewhere down the line, someone paid something, no matter where the food came from. Giving your money or donating food is by far the easiest way you can serve. Unfortunately, I saw some bad examples of this while I was on the streets. Churches would come and bring meals to us in the park. More times than not, the people were more interested in filling our stomachs the fastest way possible so they could go home. I not only saw this firsthand, but many of my homeless friends saw it, too. If you serve someone's body without ministering to his or her mind and soul, then it is highly possible that the only good you are doing is enabling him or her to continue living on the street. The only investment that serving someone's body requires is money, and that is playing it safe.

To serve the soul, we must be filled with the Holy Spirit. All Christians have access to the Holy Spirit in sharing the Gospel, but if you do not spend time in God's Word, your effectiveness to minister in this way will be diminished. Everyone's soul is going to spend eternity in either heaven or hell. Every Christian has the ability and obligation to serve the needy world with the Gospel. To minister in this way is to share God's Word with others. This is a commission for Christians to make disciples (Matthew 28:19). For example, in Woodruff Park I would often see someone sharing God's Word with everyone passing by. Sometimes it was too forceful, but nonetheless, the Gospel was getting out. It's difficult listening to someone share the Gospel when you're hungry. Ministering to the soul without ministering to the body, especially in the case of the homeless, is highly ineffective. This form of service is more difficult than giving to the body because it takes spiritual maturity and boldness. I know money is not easy to come by for some, but I have found that the boldness to share the Gospel is far more difficult to come by in American churches. However, from my experience on the streets, I saw that there is one area of service to the poor that lacked more than the others and that is the service to the mind.

The mind is a person's moral or emotional nature or sense of identity. This is what every human possesses, and this element often is overlooked while ministering to others. Churches fed me while I was on the streets, and they shared the Gospel with me seven times a week or more. From what I could see, churches gave their money and shared the Word of God, but I hate to say that far too many times, I felt like their motivation wasn't pure. Like many of my homeless friends told me, these people would feed us, but then they would pat themselves on the back and go home.

What does it take to minister to one's mind? What it takes is harder to come by than money for most. It appears to be harder to come by than simply sharing the Gospel (as hard as that may be to do sometimes). Serving one's mind requires what we rarely want to give up: our time. I don't mean a little bit of it either. If we were as interested in our heavenly investments as much as our worldly investments, don't you think that we would spend more time serving others? If you remember, Bill was a good example of this. He spent hours with me after feeding me. He opened his house up to me, but he was not a Christian. He cared for my body and my mind but not my soul. I am happy to say that there were examples of people who ministered in all three ways. Most of the times we were ministered to effectively, it was by individuals outside of a corporate church setting. Mrs. Kay and Mike are good examples, as are many people that would come sit with us while we ate at Safehouse. Those people knew our names. They knew where we were from. They gave us their contact info. They prayed with us.

These people gave to our bodies by providing food and they shared the Gospel with us to minister to our souls. They also ministered to our minds by taking the time to remember our names and look us in the eyes. They cared for our minds by telling us about their lives. They would joke with us about Mikey's ridiculous jokes. They would play cards with us. They would give us hugs. These people would spend their time doing more than getting us through the food line as fast as possible. Most of all, I could tell that they were motivated by love!

I can't tell you what to do, but I do want to challenge you to do is this: figure out what God is asking you to do and ask yourself, what am I doing to achieve that? People often ask me what I have done since my time on the streets. The answer to that question may help give you clarity on how to approach the homeless of America. I did not start a homeless ministry or a soup kitchen. I stay in contact with Mikey and John occasionally but, other than that, have very little contact with homeless people. The reason for this is because God has narrowed the focus He has for my life.

The more I study scripture, the more I see who God wants me to minister to. God wants Christians to minister to the needy. 1 John 3:17–18 says to give to those in need. James 1:27 says to take care of widows and orphans in their time of need. Luke 14:12–14 says to invite the poor to be fed. Proverbs is full of principles in regards to sharing with the poor. The list goes on and on, but the point I want to make is that the poor and needy people talked about in scripture are different than the homeless people of America. Mikey said that he was blessed because he could get water and he was not in danger of starving. Larry, Bill, and James all knew where to go to get off the streets, and they had the ability to fix their situations. The homeless people of America (for the most part) have the ability to better themselves. The widows and orphans in James chapter 1 do not. God wants me to help take care of the needy, which does not always mean the homeless people of America.

God used my experience on the street to guide me into missions. I plan on reaching an unreached group and helping to translate the Bible into their language. That is one of the greatest needs of the world—to fulfill the great commission. While I am preparing to go overseas, I still live in the states and want to help the needy. Like I told a leader at the church in Buckhead, it's about relationships. God has directed me and my family to focus on caring for a small number of people so we can invest more of our time and resources and have greater impact on fewer people. We have picked out an inner city family to minister to. We have their three children over to spend the night at our house, and we take them out to eat, along with other activities. We try to invest in them and teach them the Gospel.

After much prayer about wanting to take care of the needy in a more drastic way, my wife and I chose to be foster parents. This gives us the opportunity to truly take care of the needy of America. We are able to make a difference in people's lives that come through our home. If each capable family in churches around the world took in one orphan, can you imagine the difference it would make? I hope this gives insight to how God has used my experience to guide me, how you should approach taking care of the needy of the world, and how to best channel your efforts. May God give you discernment on your journey.

Acknowledgments

To my heavenly Father, who uses my weakness for His Glory

To my wife, Jessica, for being patient while I give up family time to complete this book and for being my first editor

To my mother and father for dealing with me in my teen years (and later)

To Nevil and Ann Smith for giving me a place to sleep and feeding me while I spent a summer writing

To Norman Naylor for making me sound better by helping me edit

To Alex Shreve and Kendall Gunter for an awesome cover

To John and Mikey, along with my other friends in Atlanta, for an unforgettable experience

To everyone who helped kick-start this project with funding—it could not have been done without you

Made in the USA
San Bernardino, CA
04 July 2017